"In a world where cyber risks are ever-evolving, *Navigating Supply Chain Cyber Risk* by Ariel Evans, Ajay Singh and Alex Golbin emerges as a vital resource. This book provides a clear and comprehensive roadmap for understanding, mitigating, and responding to third party cyber risks. Whether you're a seasoned security professional or just starting out, Evans, Singh and Golbin's insightful guidance empowers you to navigate the complex digital landscape. Here's what particularly impressed me:

- Practical and actionable: *Navigating Supply Chain Cyber Risk* goes beyond theory, offering practical steps and real-world examples to fortify your defenses.
- Accessible and engaging: The writing style is clear and engaging, making complex topics understandable for a broad audience.
- Comprehensive coverage: This book delves into a wide range of third party cyber risks, from data breaches to malware attacks, providing a holistic view of the threat landscape.

If you're looking to build a resilient and secure digital environment, *Navigating Supply Chain Cyber Risk* is a must-read."

Dr. Yoav Intrator, *Chief Product Officer, RiskQ*

"In an era where digital threats loom large over the intricate web of global supply chains, *Navigating Supply Chain Cyber Risk* emerges as a beacon of insight and practical wisdom. This book makes essential reading for anyone looking to navigate the complex intersection of supply chain management and cybersecurity. With its clear explanations, real-world examples, and actionable strategies, it equips professionals with requisite tools to protect their critical operations against cyber threats. A timely and valuable contribution to the field."

Nagendra Aswatha, *Asst. Professor, Operations & Supply Chain Management*

NAVIGATING SUPPLY CHAIN CYBER RISK

Cybersecurity is typically viewed as the boogeyman, and vendors are responsible for 63% of reported data breaches in organisations. And as businesses grow, they will use more and more third parties to provide specialty services. Typical cybersecurity training programs focus on phishing awareness and email hygiene. This is not enough. *Navigating Supply Chain Cyber Risk: A Comprehensive Guide to Managing Third Party Cyber Risk* helps companies establish cyber vendor risk management programs and understand cybersecurity in its true context from a business perspective.

The concept of cybersecurity until recently has revolved around protecting the perimeter. Today we know that the concept of the perimeter is dead. The corporate perimeter in cyber terms is no longer limited to the enterprise alone, but extends to its business partners, associates, and third parties that connect to its IT systems. This book, written by leaders and cyber risk experts in business, is based on three years of research with the Fortune 1000 and cyber insurance industry carriers, reinsurers, and brokers and the collective wisdom and experience of the authors in Third Party Risk Management, and serves as a ready reference for developing policies, procedures, guidelines, and addressing evolving compliance requirements related to vendor cyber risk management. It is unique since it provides strategies and learnings that have shown to lower risk and demystify cyber risk when dealing with third and fourth parties.

The book is essential reading for CISOs, DPOs, CPOs, Sourcing Managers, Vendor Risk Managers, Chief Procurement Officers, Cyber Risk Managers, Compliance Managers, and other cyber stakeholders, as well as students in cyber security.

Ariel Evans is a senior cybersecurity expert, serial entrepreneur, and award-winning author. She is the chairperson of the cybersecurity continuing education programs at Seton Hall University and Pace University and has been on the front lines of cybersecurity as a former CISO, and Cyber Risk Manager.

Ajay Singh is a Professor of Practice, corporate advisor, Fellow at the Institute of Directors, Former CEO, and award-winning author.

Alex Golbin is a Senior Financial Services Executive with over two decades of leading Risk Management, Enterprise Resiliency, Operations and Technology Transformation, Global Technology, Business Process Improvement, and leveraging state-of-the-art technology.

NAVIGATING SUPPLY CHAIN CYBER RISK

A Comprehensive Guide to Managing Third Party Cyber Risk

Ariel Evans, Ajay Singh and Alex Golbin

Routledge
Taylor & Francis Group

LONDON AND NEW YORK

Designed cover image: Suphanat Khumsap / iStock / Getty Images Plus

First published 2025
by Routledge
4 Park Square, Milton Park, Abingdon, Oxon OX14 4RN

and by Routledge
605 Third Avenue, New York, NY 10158

Routledge is an imprint of the Taylor & Francis Group, an informa business

British Library Cataloguing-in-Publication Data
A catalogue record for this book is available from the British Library

ISBN: 978-1-032-94762-4 (hbk)
ISBN: 978-1-032-94761-7 (pbk)
ISBN: 978-1-003-58132-1 (ebk)

DOI: 10.4324/9781003581321

Typeset in Joanna
by codeMantra

CONTENTS

ABOUT THE AUTHORS

Ariel Evans is a senior cybersecurity expert, serial entrepreneur, and award-winning author. Ariel is a professor at Pace University and leads an advisory board of over 170 CISOs, CTOs, CIOs, DPOs, Cyber Attorneys, and Insurance Firms in research into Cyber Risk Management. Her books and courses are based upon seven years of research with the Fortune 1000 and cyber insurance industry.

Ariel is the pioneer of the digital asset approach to cyber risk. Her most recent product company, RiskQ has patented the digital asset approach and created a cyber risk quantification platform called ValuRisQ for organizations, InsurQ for insurance companies, and RadarQ for IT asset management.

She also founded in 2018, Cyber Intelligence 4U (CIU). CIU is a cyber education services company that provides leading courses for universities, organizations, and individuals focused on filling the gaps in traditional education that are needed to meet the challenges of the digital age. CIU works with Pace University, Seton Hall University, Rutgers University, ISACA, and others. Over 4000 students have gone through the programs in 2018. Clients include Verizon, AM Best, Citibank, and a host of others.

She has won numerous awards including the EU Commission award for Innovation in cyber risk and Gartner Cool Vendor in Privacy Management.

Formerly, she was a founder of two software companies in the United States that were spun and sold to BMC and elance.com, a Kleiner Perkins company. Additionally, she was the Acting Chief Information Security Officer for a Telco subsidiary in the United States and was responsible for the establishment of the Information Security division, from the very initial stage of defining the security and compliance requirements to the assimilation of IT security and compliance programs across the firm. She was accountable for IT security policies and procedures, governance and standardization of all security and compliance-related IT activities and risk management.

Ariel has sat on the board as a cyber expert for several companies. Her insight into regulation, governance, and business connectivity technology allows Ariel to provide expert guidance to the Department of Homeland Security, the Payment Card Industry and other governing bodies that are accountable for reducing risk and ensuring secure financial, medical and personal data. Ariel is the primary author of the PCI Security Council e-commerce guidelines issued in January of 2013.

Ariel has her undergraduate degree in Nuclear Physics and her M.B.A. from New York University's Stern School of Business.

Books

Managing Cyber Risk – A Cyber Risk Managers' Handbook, ISBN-13: 978-0367177737. Bit.ly/ArielEvans.

Enterprise Cybersecurity in Digital Business; – Building a Resilient Organization. ISBN-13: 978-0367511494. https://amzn.to/39CvR7h. Awarded Top 30 Cybersecurity Books you should read in 2024.

Cybersecurity and AI for Business: in development.

Articles

Contributor to the Cybersecurity Law Review.
How CISOs Can Use Digital Asset Metrics to Tell a Coherent Cyber Story to the Board.
How Much Cyber Insurance to Buy Based on How Claims Are Paid.

Media

Women in Cyber Interview: https://crri.us/international-women-in-cyber-ariel-evans/?fbclid=IwAR0OadPlBkZrKQ6M4oKV01kVz9gc1oRJB_d3Br22wiUgmZfp0ZeBDRP8JjU.

Task Force 7 Radio (Top 10 podcasts): https://www.voiceamerica.com/guest/44210/
ariel-evans.

The James Bohannon Show: http://www.jimbohannonshow.com/2018/03/15/
wednesday-march-14-2018/.

I24 News interview on GDPR and Cyber Risk: https://www.youtube.com/watch?
v=LfctYo2Wyw4&t=34s.

Memberships and Chairs

Chairperson of the Pace Academic Advisory Board-Pace University-Seidenberg School
of Computer Science and Information Systems, New York.

Chairperson of the Seton Hall Academic Advisory Board-Pace University-Seidenberg
School of Computer Science and Information Systems, New Jersey.

Member of the International Association of Privacy Professionals (IAPP).

Member of the Information Systems Audit and Control Association (ISACA).

Member of the Cloud Security Alliance (CSA).

Ajay Singh is Professor of Practice, corporate advisor, Fellow at the Institute
of Directors, former CEO, and award-winning author.

Memberships

Member of IEEE Committee on Cyber Security for Next Generation Connectivity
Systems.

Member of the Academic Advisory Board-Pace University-Seidenberg School of
Computer Science and Information Systems, New York.

Books

Cyber Strong: A Primer on Cyber Risk Management for Business Managers (2020): This book was
recognized as an Award-Winning Finalist at the International Book Awards by the
American Book Fest in 2022.

An Entrepreneur's IOD Handbook on Cyber Security (2021): A condensed guide tailored for
corporate professionals and executive management.

Cybersecurity-Concepts, Principles, Technologies, and Practices (2023): This work has received the
prestigious Golden Book Award in 2024.

Cyber Strong: Cybersecurity and Risk Management (2023).

Cyber Shock: Cyber-Attacks that Shook the World (2024). An exploration of significant cyber
incidents and the lessons we can learn from them.

Alex Golbin is a senior financial services executive with over two decades of leading Risk Management, Regulatory Remediation, Enterprise Resiliency, Operations and Technology Transformation, Global Technology, Risk and Control Functions, Data, Business Process Improvement, and leveraging state-of-the-art technology.

Alex's current and prior roles included leadership responsibilities in numerous globally recognized Fortune 500 Companies, including global systemically important banks.

In one of his prior roles Alex led a Vendor Risk Assessments business (as part of a joint venture with 16 Banks and Financial Services companies) to improve operational resilience, regulatory compliance, and cost. He has successfully led the enablement of multiple global industry consortiums, industry risk management & cybersecurity frameworks, and the establishment of strategic industry partnerships.

Memberships

Member of the Information Systems Audit and Control Association (ISACA).

Member of the Project Management Institute (PMI).

Member of the Academic Advisory Board-Pace University-Seidenberg School of Computer Science and Information Systems, New York.

Certifications

Project Management Professional (PMP).

Certified Data Privacy Solutions Engineer (CDPSE).

Certified Information Security Manager (CISM).

Alex has an MBA from NYU Stern in Finance and Management, BS in Computer Science. He serves on multiple advisory boards as an expert in cybersecurity, risk management, and technology.

PREFACE

Cybersecurity is the number one business risk according to Forbes. Seventy percent of data breaches are due to third parties. As a result of this interdependency between organizations and their vendors, we are writing this book to help organizations address this urgent need to evaluate their supply chain and understand the potential cyber consequences for each of their third parties.

The security of a company is only as strong as its weakest link. Over the past five years there has been an emphasis on understanding the role that third parties play in cybersecurity. Not only what role they play, but also an increase in focus from regulatory bodies. Today, almost every cybersecurity, privacy, and industry regulation has language that addresses the requirements of the third party.

This book is written as a comprehensive guide to understand, manage, and mitigate third-party cyber risks. It will provide you with the knowledge and tools you need to protect your organization's supply chain regardless of if you have an existing program or are you just starting from scratch.

We begin the book, providing background research into the impacts, and trends, using case studies and examples to embed your learning experience. We follow that up with regulatory data that is critical to understanding the requirements your company faces with third parties. We then begin the how-to section that walks the reader through preparation, due diligence, policies, risk quantification, risk scoring, and audit.

We summarize our thoughts on the future in the way forward focusing on AI.

Cyber risk management is a journey without a destination. We will always have cyber risk. It is a journey of managing it with the best chances of success. May your journey be one of wonder, growth, and resilience.

ACKNOWLEDGMENTS

No book writes itself and no author can share knowledge without standing on the shoulder of giants. We wish to express our heartfelt thanks and appreciation to our colleagues, friends, researchers, and mentors who have helped us to frame our thoughts and complete this book.

A special thanks to all two hundred members of the Pace Seidenberg Cybersecurity Advisory Board, whose amazing collaboration has helped to make this book possible. There are too many of you to thank individually.

A hearty thanks to Dean Jonathan Hill from Pace University's Seidenberg School of Computer Science and Information Systems.

From the team: We are all passionate about supply chain cyber risk, being on both sides of the equation and seeing the struggle over the past several years to have strong programs to understand the cyber risks, program requirements, and regulations. This book is meant to move people forward, faster based on our work in this area.

From Ariel: I cannot forget to triple thank my husband again and again. Doctor Yoav Intrator who is bar none an expert in technology innovation, AI and in all things cyber and whose example propels me to excel, for his support, wisdom, and his unconditional belief in love in me. You are my rock.

From Alex: It was an exciting journey to publish this book, to distill nuances and complexity of this most important and complex risk to the industry. As part of the creative experience, I appreciated the friendship and bond I formed with my two co-authors, learning from each other, and making something that we can all be proud of. I want to especially thank my family Alice, Abigail, and Aaron for supporting me during this journey, the countless weekends of calls, writing, and blabbering about obscure topics around cybersecurity.

From Ajay: Collaborating with Ariel and Alex on this book was incredibly rewarding. We brought diverse expertise to the table, and our brainstorming sessions sparked innovative ideas. The camaraderie and shared passion for our topic made the process enjoyable. A special thanks to my lovely wife, Sangeeta for her unwavering support.

We hope you find this book useful.

PART I

THE CASE FOR SUPPLY CHAIN CYBER RISK MANAGEMENT

1

THE EXTENDED ENTERPRISE

Introduction

In 2018, Dr. Yoav Intrator, the former CEO of JPMorgan Chase Israel, published a paper titled "An Autonomous Economy: Coming Sooner Than You Think."[1] The paper focused on how responsibilities are shifting from human to machine and was the first to formally define autonomous economy (AE) as an IT-driven economy.

In the AE paper, he identified four key barriers, **Trust, Supply Chain, Regulation,** and **Platform** to reach an autonomous state. He also referred to them as frictions, since on the surface they slow us down in moving from an IT-enabled economy to an IT-driven economy. However, at the same time, they are innovation triggers which drive innovation; social, technological, and economic frictions stimulate invention. This book will explore one of these frictions, supply chain, from a cyber risk perspective and the risk it poses as an extended enterprise.

In the past few years, we have observed how the four identified frictions are being amplified. The increase in fake news erodes our trust, and the emerging

DOI: 10.4324/9781003581321-2

crisis in the world supply chain stifles our growth. The increase in regulations is costly and challenging to comply with in response to the growth in cyber-attacks and fraud, and the continued growth in demand to fulfill communications, storage, and computation needs puts pressure on the current platforms, all who race to address innovation in the face of these frictions.

Cybersecurity risk is embedded in each of the four frictions. It is the key to measuring trust. Data integrity addresses data trustworthiness. Cyber is an interconnected discipline and each organization is only as secure as their weakest supply chain link – as we painfully were reminded after the SolarWinds hack.

In 2019, Jamie Dimon, the Chairperson and CEO of JPMorgan Chase, stated that "The threat of cybersecurity may very well be the biggest threat to the U.S (United States). financial system."[2]

Cybersecurity-related risks are the #1 business issue[3] and have led to a growing discipline: Cyber Risk Quantification and Management. Cyber Risk is a digital science that focuses on the quantification of financial impacts and likelihoods of a cyber event. It amplifies reputation harm, productivity losses, and legal issues due to the failure to protect the digital assets.

Third-party cyber risk (also synonymously called vendor or supply chain) is in the headlines every day. Third parties are compelled contractually and by law to report data breaches to their customers and to the regulators.

Third-party cyber risk can be quantified and analyzed based on the digital Information Technology (IT) assets the vendor is interacting with. Vendors may process and store data in cloud services, build ITs, or systems and/or work with data. The ability to measure vendor cyber risk is related to how they cause risk. Cloud service providers (CSPs) process and store data. The risk to the first party is related to a data breach. The first party is required by law to notify their customers of data breaches. The cost of a third-party data breach is typically three times that of an on-premise data breach. The vendor is also measured based on the likelihood that they have effective cyber policies, people, controls, and tools.

Unprecedented Velocity in Digital IT Assets

Businesses assets have been shifting rapidly from the physical world into the digital arena and, in doing so, have increased the attack surface exponentially. In 2001, only 10% of business assets were digital IT assets. Today it is over 85%.[4]

What this means is that to improve, maintain, or restore trust, we must protect our digital IT assets. Digital assets are ubiquitous. As our digital asset attack surface grows, so do the challenges in protecting them. Cyber criminals target our digital assets. They steal data, interrupt business processes with ransomware, and in many cases, they expose regulatory incompliance that can result in fines and penalties.

Privacy regulation is exploding. Privacy programs are similar to cybersecurity programs. There are two major differences. (1) They only address privacy data. (2) They have additional use and collection of data requirements. Below are some key statistics and trends, which highlight the importance of Cyber Risk as a discipline and how they tie to the emergence of privacy programs.

The cyber regulatory velocity has increased over 950% in the past six years,[5] and it is likely to double in the next 5 years when all 50 states are expected to have privacy laws. Cyber regulation requires cyber expertise. CCPA (California Consumer Privacy Act), GDPR (General Data Protection Regulation), CPA (Colorado Privacy Act) (Colorado Privacy NAIC (National Association of Insurance Commissioners), NYSDFS Part 500, NAIC (National Association of Insurance Commissioners) Model Law and over 20 nation-state laws all require cyber programs. All cybersecurity and privacy laws *require a vendor risk management program*. Furthermore, all 50 states are expected to have privacy laws that require both *first- and third-party cyber programs* (Figure 1.1).

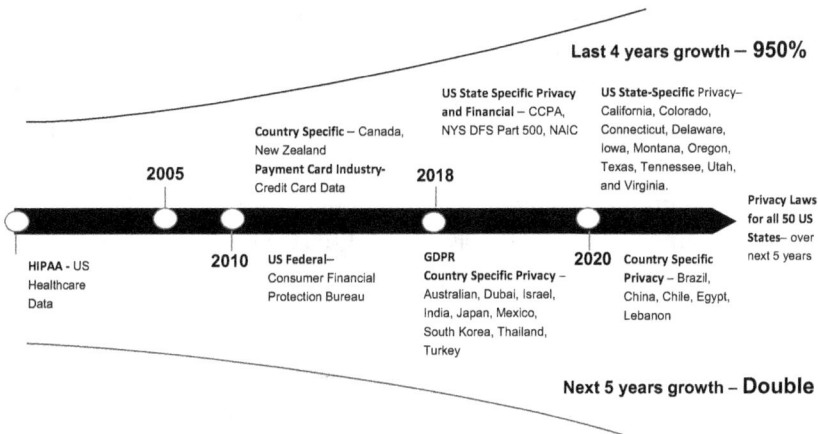

Figure 1.1 Regulatory Velocity 2018 to Present is 950%

Trust as an Asset

Beyond the bottom-line financial impact of cybercrime, the biggest impact of cyber risk is a reduction in Trust. This is especially true in the Financial Industry. Cybercrime has a devastating impact on the only asset that banks hold and cannot trade with – TRUST. In general, reduction of trust has a long-tail impact which includes loss of market cap, employees, and legal implications.

Cyber and the Supply Chain

Understanding supply chain and its relationship to cyber risk is the key to not only complying with regulations but also to defining who is responsible to protecting those digital assets. Trust is related to supply chain. Let us explore how. If you use a cloud service provider, you share the responsibility to protect your digital assets that they either process or store on your behalf. While data owners are relieved from maintaining the physical infrastructure, when it comes to risk, the reality is that the data owner carries more of the financial risk. A CSP is a vendor and a large part of our supply chain. The important aspect of measuring supply chain trust is to understand how to quantify the financial risk and know which party is responsible for which cyber controls and measuring their effectiveness.

Common sense suggests that we cannot treat a CSP the same way we treat a management consulting firm, outside counsel, or accountants when it comes to cyber risk. These are service providers, not IT infrastructure providers. We also cannot treat on-premise system vendor like a CSP. It is crucial to understand the context of how each vendor works with our digital assets and their associated risk implications. System providers provide technologies that are specific business solutions. Look at SolarWinds. SolarWinds is an infrastructure and security management system. What was not understood was the business context – SolarWinds must have rock-solid development practices to prevent the insertion of malware in their updates.

Until we understand our supply chain in the context of our digital assets, we cannot manage our third-party cyber risk, which is required by cyber law!

Cyber Crime Is Like the Covid-19 Virus

We are in an economy where the rate of new vulnerabilities is growing every year. In 2023 there were 26,447 new vulnerabilities[6] reported.

That is more than 72 vulnerabilities a day, which suggests that businesses must continuously assess and quantify their cyber risk exposure, and continuously evaluate their plans and priorities to remediate critical vulnerabilities.

Cybercrime is like the COVID-19 virus. The virus continuously mutates in response to our best efforts, with businesses having to endlessly figure out how to rise above it. It is here to stay, and it will continue to increase the financial risks to our businesses. Your vendor's vulnerabilities are your vulnerabilities.

Lack of Quantifiable Metrics Must Be Tied to Cyber Investment

There seems to never be enough money to protect digital assets. JPMorgan reported in 2015 10-Q reports its intention to invest half a billion in cyber, doubling their investment from the previous year. In 2018, three years later, the firm reported spending US$600 million on cybersecurity. At this rate one will not be surprised if this year there is a US$1B investment in cybersecurity.

Understanding the return on investment and the reduction of financial exposure goes a long way to justifying cyber budgets. Five percent of IT spending has nothing to do with cyber risk. It is time to stop using math that does not work.

Recommendations for Boards and Senior Corporate Leaders

It is not a question of if but of when. Botnets spread automatically and are geographically and industry agnostic. Cyber extortion, data exfiltration, malware, and ransomware impact the business' ability to meet quarterly projections. Each data breach results in over 31% of the firm being fired or leaving.

This business reality clearly requires risk quantification to demonstrate return on investment and risk reduction. Using a quantified cyber risk solution allows the firm to understand the effectiveness of their vendor's controls and manage their own risk objectively.

Every board and executive should be able to answer the following vendor questions.

- How much third-party cyber risk exposure do we have?
- Which vendors pose the most financial risk to us?
- How do we prioritize our vendor risk reduction?
- How do we optimize our organizational model and processes to better address vendor risk?
- How can we have a unified view of cyber risk that allows for a common ontology?
- How can we help our vendors protect us?

As we march into an autonomous economy, cyber, with all its implications on trust, supply chain risk, innovation driven by increasing regulation realizes that corporations must quickly adopt cyber risk best practices and tools. It is not an option anymore; it is necessary.

Notes

1   Intrator, Y. (2018, January). Autonomous economy: Coming sooner than you think. Technology Insights Global. https://www.researchgate.net/publication/346790343_Technology_INSIGHTS_GLOBAL_Autonomous_Economy_Coming_Sooner_Than_You_Think.
2   Son, H. (2019, April 4). Jamie Dimon says risk of cyberattacks "may be biggest threat to the US financial system." CNBC. https://www.cnbc.com/2019/04/04/jp-morgan-ceo-jamie-dimon-warns-cyber-attacks-biggest-threat-to-us.html#:~:text=tied%20to%20hackers.-,%E2%80%9CThe%20threat%20of%20cyber%20security%20may%20very%20well%20be%20the,the%20business%2C%E2%80%9D%20Dimon%20said.
3   Ariel Evans, MetLife, 2021 presentation.
4   Katsiri, R. (2020, February 2). JP Morgan to step up investment in Israel. Globes. https://en.globes.co.il/en/article-jp-morgan-to-step-up-investment-in-israel-1001317017.
5   Ariel Evans, MetLife, 2021 presentation.
6   Abbasi, S. (2024, January 4). 2023 Threat landscape year in review: If everything is critical, nothing is. Qualys. https://blog.qualys.com/vulnerabilities-threat-research/2023/12/19/2023-threat-landscape-year-in-review-part-one#:~:text=MITRE%20ATT%26CK%20tactics.-,2023%20Statistics,found%20than%20the%20year%20before.

2

KNOW YOUR SUPPLY CHAIN

First, Second, Third, and Fourth Parties

The first party is your company and all the on-premise digital assets. As you learned earlier, this risk is the exposures[1] and the likelihood that your company will have a data breach or cyber event.[2]

Second-party cyber risk comes from your customers or members. Customers or members can log into your systems and touch your digital assets. Customers may not have antivirus, or other security measures, on devices, making it easier for hackers to gain access to your data.

A third party is an institution or person to which you outsource an activity. There are several types of third parties. Cloud service providers who store and process your data and provide you with software, infrastructure, or a platform as a service. Service vendors who provide management, IT, legal, accounting, or other services. Also included are technology vendors who you buy technologies from and system vendors who you buy systems from. Each must be understood in context.

DOI: 10.4324/9781003581321-3

Unless a contract specifically forbids it, a vendor can transfer its rights and responsibilities to a fourth party.

Your institution outsources to third parties and those vendors outsource to other vendors. These are called fourth parties. This relates to your vendors' third-party cyber risk management program.

Your firm owns the data it collects and is accountable to protect it. Your institution is also responsible for the life of that data when it is stored or processed by a third party. Consequently, your firm is also responsible for the activities of your vendors' third-party vendors (aka your fourth-party vendors). The more your third parties outsource to other vendors, the greater the costs and risks of vendor management.

The Statement on Standards for Attestation Engagements 18 (SSAE 18)[3] has a vendor management requirement that states you must define the scope and responsibilities of each third-party vendor you use, address security assessment findings, audits, and monitoring.

Vendors that have access to sensitive data put your firm at risk of a data breach. Other key concerns of the vendor portfolio include those that perform critical business services, interact with customers, or perform a sensitive, highly publicized function that exposes your firm to reputational risk.

Know Your Supply Chain

Just as Know Your Client (KYC) is a set of standards used in the investment services industry to verify customers and their risk and financial profiles, Know Your Supply Chain is equally important. The three components of Know Your Supply Chain are:

1. Supply Chain Vendor Identification (SCVI). The first step in KYSC processes is to identify the vendors that are a part of your supply chain. This requires a technical understanding of what the supply chain vendor does for your business.
2. Vendor Due Diligence (VDD). Vendor Due Diligence takes identification further and asks whether you can trust the vendor. Most firms rely on procurement for this function; however in the case of cyber risk, it is advisable to have the technical team owning this function working tangentially with procurement. For all supply chain vendors involved, identifying what type of vendor they are (CSP, System, Technology, or Service Provider) and their importance must be determined since they have different types of risk.

Cloud service provider risk is based on how well they are protecting your data. System and Technology vendor risk is based on how well they protect their updates from malware. Service provider risk is based on the human factor and how well they train their personnel in cybersecurity.

VDD is about establishing a vendor's risk level and to what extent they can be trusted.

There are three levels of VDD based on their types: Cloud, System/Technology, and Service Provider.

- Cloud Service Due Diligence. For cloud service providers, the controls that are owned by the cloud service and those that are owned by the company must be documented and assessed.
- System and Vendor Due Diligence. On the other hand, technology and system vendors provide technical solutions that must be verified as malware free.
- Service Provider Vendor Due Diligence. Service providers like accountants and lawyers must have background checks, security awareness training and align to the cybersecurity rules of your firm.

3. Ongoing Monitoring.

KYSC is not just about checking new suppliers during onboarding. This is important, of course, and will establish the identity and initial risk level of the customer, but cybersecurity risk programs must have ongoing checks and monitoring.

Ongoing monitoring will identify changes in customer activity that may warrant an adjustment in their cyber risk profile or further investigation. The level and frequency of monitoring will depend on the customer's perceived risk and the institution's strategy.

- Monitoring should look at factors including:
- Annual assessments
- Changes in supplier transaction types, frequency, and amounts
- Changes in supplier locations
- Adverse media coverage due to a cyber event

As with the previous two KYSC components, SCVI and VDD, companies should have well-established processes in place to handle ongoing monitoring. This should include the raising of concerns relating to suspicious activity.

Types of Supply Chain Vendors

Third parties must be considered in their true context. A Cloud Service Provider is much different than a management consultant or an attorney.

Cloud Service Providers – A cloud service provider is a third-party company offering a cloud-based platform, infrastructure, application, or storage services. There are several types.

- SaaS (software as a service) provides software as a service where software is licensed on a subscription basis and is centrally hosted.
- PaaS (platform as a service) provides a platform as a service that allows clients to develop, run, and manage applications without the complexity of building and maintaining the infrastructure typically associated with developing and launching an application.
- IaaS (infrastructure as a service) provides infrastructure as a service in an instant computing infrastructure, provisioned and managed over the internet. Each resource is offered as a separate service component. Customers rent a particular service component for only as long as it is needed. Microsoft Azure is an example. Microsoft manages the infrastructure, the customer purchases, installs, configures, and manages their own software, operating systems, middleware, and applications.

Most of these models also provide data storage.

Service Providers – A third-party organization that provides services to the company. Examples include lawyers, accountants, doctors, IT companies, management consultants, etc.

System Vendors – Third-party organizations that provide a set of technologies that are sold as a system.

Technology Vendors – Third parties that sell technologies such as databases, frameworks, languages, security tools, etc.

Vendor Teams

Cyber Vendor Risk Management is becoming its own discipline. It is ideal if there is a centralized vendor or procurement team responsible for cyber risk. Team members will include the security team, internal security assessors (ISAs), legal team, and business owners. The procurement team ideally is the project management team that understands the requirements and reports on the program's effectiveness. The ISAs typically collect cybersecurity evidence that will be acceptable to the firm. The security team helps to define the cybersecurity requirements and ensure that the vendor team understands what is required for the vendor to comply with third-party programs. The legal team will review the contract. Once the vendor has provided a risk assessment, the ISAs will review the evidence and discuss the results with the vendor team. Business owners provide input to key functions and vendor requirements across the firm.

Vendor Contracts

A vendor's cybersecurity due diligence should begin prior to working with a firm. All vendors should establish and maintain a cyber risk strategy. This is a documented program strategy for identifying and managing cybersecurity risks. An organization's cybersecurity strategy will be driven by laws and regulations that the organization is subject to, applicable industry standards, and the organization's assessment of its own tolerance for risk. Certain laws will mandate specific terms for vendor agreements. As an example, the Health Insurance Portability and Accounting Act (HIPAA) requires a Business Associate Agreement. The US government has contract provisions in vendor agreements for companies doing business with the EU. This includes the Privacy Shield Principles.

Vendors that use subcontractors and suppliers (fourth parties) who may have access to your systems and data must have adequate third-party programs. *Your vendor contracts must require an assignment clause which provides your firm notice and consent before the vendor outsources any part of the contract.* This gives a firm the ability to control fourth-party risk.

A digital asset inventory should be done of the data, systems, and business processes that the vendor will work with at the organization. Likewise, the organization should have an inventory of the systems and technologies the vendor is providing as well as the type of data to be processed or stored by the vendor.

Analyzing the digital asset interconnectivity and dependencies with the third parties is an element of starting a cybersecurity risk assessment.

Organizations should evaluate the inherent cybersecurity risk of people, processes, technology, and data that support an identified function. Companies must assess the effectiveness of cybersecurity controls to protect against the identified risk. Cyber risk assessments provide the basis for the application of appropriate controls and the development of remediation plans to mitigate risks and vulnerabilities down to a reasonable and appropriate level.[4]

Vendor Risk Assessment Program

Vendor risk assessment programs must be fit for purpose. Typical steps to set up a vendor risk assessment program include:

1. Vendor digital asset inventory and identification of vendor type(s).
   - Identification of digital asset goods or services provided in relationship to data that will be processed or stored by the vendor.
   - The type of access to systems given to a vendor and why.
   - The digital asset supported by the vendor.
   - Criticality of business service supported by the vendor.
   - The nature of the service provided by the vendor and determination if the vendor directly interacts with your customers or handles other client-facing activities.
2. Identification of regulation(s) or industry standard(s) for the vendor to abide by.
   - Mapping of requirements across different regulations to reduce redundancy.
   - Ensure that the compliance program is aligned to applicable federal, state, and local laws.
3. Creation of a Vendor Questionnaire or automated control evaluation related to vendor type.
   - Ensure specific requirements are included in vendor questionnaires (i.e., ciphers required for encryption, etc.) or automated control evaluation.
   - Include fourth-party requirements.
   - Select a framework and ensure at a minimum:
     - Review of security policies and procedures and the enforcement of the vendor's security policies.
     - Effective incident response and business continuity/disaster recovery.
     - Table-top exercises of DR plans are tested regularly and updated.

- Secure Software Development Life Cycle (SSDLC).
- Latest vulnerability scan.
- Latest pen test.
- Threat intelligence tools and processes.
- Disclosure of incidents/breaches and vulnerabilities the vendor identified in the vendor's systems.

4. Vendor Questionnaire and Control Evidence Review
   - Independent control attestations.
   - Review evidence with ISA Team.
5. Vendor Cyber Risk Profile Review
   - Determine data exfiltration and inherent vendor cyber risk.
6. Monitoring of vendor based on risk profile.

Notes

1 Jones, D. (2023, February 2). 98% of organizations worldwide have connected to breached third-party vendors. *Cybersecurity Dive.* https://www.cybersecuritydive.com/news/connected-breached-third-party/641857/#:~:text=A%20total%20of%2098%25%20of,SecurityScorecard%20and%20the%20Cyentia%20Institute.

2 Statista (2024). Average cost of a data breach in the United States from 2006 to 2023. https://www.statista.com/statistics/273575/us-average-cost-incurred-by-a-data-breach/#:~:text=As%20of%202023%2C%20the%20average,million%20U.S.%20dollars%20in%202023. Wikipedia (2020, December 1). SSAE No. 18. https://en.wikipedia.org/wiki/SSAE_No._18.

3 Whittaker, Z. (2020, January 30). Social media boosting service exposed thousands of Instagram passwords. *TechCrunch.* https://techcrunch.com/2020/01/30/social-captain-instagram-passwords/.

4 Whittaker, Z. (2020, January 30). Social media boosting service exposed thousands of Instagram passwords. *TechCrunch.* https://techcrunch.com/2020/01/30/social-captain-instagram-passwords/.

3

NOTABLE SUPPLY CHAIN CYBER EVENTS

Managing Supply Chain Risks-Issues

Organizations in recent years have enhanced their capabilities in managing cyber threats and associated risks making it difficult for threat actors to gain access to their critical systems and data. Meanwhile, threat actors have upped their game by discovering a new attack vector through third parties as they can exploit the trust and dependency that organizations have on third-party software or services. Third parties include organizations or individuals who provide services or products to another organization, such as vendors, contractors, partners, suppliers, cloud providers, etc. Inevitably this dependence on third parties can expose an organization to cyber risks in several ways, such as:

- Sharing access to sensitive data or organization systems with third parties who may not have the required security measures or policies in place.

DOI: 10.4324/9781003581321-4

- Continuing the use of open source, outdated, or legacy software from third parties which is not supported anymore by them.
- Outsourcing critical functions or processes to third parties who may not comply with the organization's standards or regulations.
- Being exposed to cyber threats such as ransomware, data theft, sabotage, espionage, and other malicious actions of threat actors who target organizations via third parties associated with them.

Regulators and government authorities have taken note of the rising number of threats organizations face via their service providers and supply chain partners and have introduced guidelines which force them to adopt a holistic and proactive approach to supply chain security to prevent or mitigate impacts from supply chain cyber-attacks. Examples of important regulations include the US Presidential Executive Order 14028 and the HIPAA (Business Associate Agreement) that incorporate provisions that organizations must implement to prevent supply chain cyber-attacks. Frameworks such as the ISO 27001 and the NIST SP 800-161 Revision 1 offer guidelines and best practices for identifying, assessing, and responding to cybersecurity risks throughout the supply chain at all levels of an organization. Prioritizing supply chain security is not just about compliance; it is about building a resilient, trustworthy, and efficient organization. By addressing vulnerabilities and managing risks, organizations can safeguard their operations and maintain a strong cybersecurity posture.

Managing cyber risk across the modern-day extended enterprise is a task that requires a clear focus and execution strategy. Key issues that organizations need to address in this context include the following:

- Organizations have limited visibility into systems and networks of supply chain participants. They also have little control over the security practices and policies of their suppliers and vendors.
- Supply chain participants have different levels of cybersecurity involving multiple types of users, processes, and technologies, each with their own security requirements and vulnerabilities.
- Supply chains are highly interdependent and interconnected. This means that a security breach in one part of the chain can have cascading effects on other parts, and potentially disrupt the entire supply chain.

- Evolving threats and technologies, such as ransomware, artificial intelligence, cloud computing, and the Internet of Things and the introduction of 5G pose new challenges and risks for supply chain security that require constant evaluation and adaptation.
- The use of third party and open-source components by supply chain participants requires conducting regular audits and scans of their codebase to identify and inventory all components and their vulnerabilities, and dependencies.
- Supply chains are often located in multiple countries and legal jurisdictions which could have conflicting regulations and laws regarding cybersecurity, data protection, and privacy. Ensuring compliance with diverse regulations and laws can be very challenging and costly, and non-compliance can lead to fines, penalties, or other legal actions.

Notable Supply Chain Cyber-Attacks

Among the early instances of supply chain cyber-attacks are the Target attack of 2013, the Home Depot breach of 2014, and the NotPetya of 2017 attack which involved using a novel method of piggy backing on a software update of a Ukrainian software company to spread the NotPetya malware.

Target (2013) – One of the Earliest Supply Chain Attacks

Target the retail giant operates a chain of discount department stores and hypermarkets across the United States of America. It is a Fortune 500 company (ranked 32 in 2022). Target had provided their heating, ventilation, and air conditioning (HVAC) contractor Fazio Mechanical Services, a Sharpsburg, Penn.-based company access to their network so that they could monitor temperatures in stores and minimize energy consumption. They were also required to alert store managers if temperatures in their stores fluctuated beyond the acceptable range that could cause any discomfort to customers from shopping at the store.

Hackers used credentials stolen from Fazio Mechanical Services to gain access to Target's network. They then installed malware on several point-of-sale (POS) systems which enabled them to capture card data from customers' transactions. The total haul for the hackers included information relating to 70 million customers and 40 million credit and debit card details. According to some estimates, the breach cost Target about US$200 million in direct expenses and US$18.5 million in settlements with states and financial institutions.[1]

Home Depot (2014) – How a Third-Party Vendor Led to the Biggest PoS Breach in History

In April 2014, hackers infiltrated Home Depot's systems by using a stolen password from a Home Depot vendor to pull off another big retail credit card breach in US history. This time the hackers could not get access to the cash registers manned by employees but succeeded in exfiltrating data from 7,500 self-checkout terminals.[2] In all, they gained access to 56 million Home Depot credit card customers as well as 53 million customer email addresses.[3] These two incidents led the card companies to move to chip-and-pin-based card system from the erstwhile magnetic strip cards.

NotPetya (2017) – How NotPetya Wiped Out Data Across the Globe Using a Compromised Software Update

In 2017, the notorious NotPetya malware designed to erase the files completely and spread rapidly across networks using various exploits and methods was mainly targeted at organizations in Ukraine even though its impact was felt in other countries as well. Threat actors chose what was at that time a novel strategy of spreading the NotPetya malware via a software update of a Ukrainian software company called MeDoc which provided tax and accounting software to many government and private organizations. This strategy (of infecting a software update to spread the malware) was later to be replicated in other prominent attacks such as SolarWinds and Kaseya (detailed later in this chapter).

CCleaner (2017) – Hackers Plant Backdoor in CCleaner Software

CCleaner is one of the oldest tools to clean a Personal Computer by removing potentially unwanted files and invalid Windows Registry entries. Threat actors inserted malware into an update which was downloaded by about 2.27 million users of the software developed by Piriform Software.

Furthermore, they enabled the threat actors to collect information from the infected devices and even execute further commands.

General Electric (2020): Third-Party Data Breach of a Fortune 500 Conglomerate

General electric (GE) has been at the forefront of innovation and is known for having spurred world-transforming changes and improved the lives of billions of people. Many consider it as a pioneer in out-sourcing and leveraging the power of their supply chain to drive efficiencies and reduce cost.

In early February 2020, one of their third-party service providers, Cannon Business Process Services (CBPS) suffered a data breach which resulted in the exposure of personal information including direct deposit forms and tax forms related to GE current and former employees.

The information that was exposed included names, addresses, social security numbers, driver's license numbers, passport details, birth, marriage, and death certificates, and other benefits application forms.

Cannon Business Process Services, a subsidiary of Cannon USA which provides operations management, workflow improvement, technology, and automation services suffered the data breach due to an email breach of one of its employee's email accounts which led to hackers gaining access to its workflow system.

It seems likely that the hackers used a simple phishing attack or a key logger to steal the email login password of the compromised account. In hindsight it can be said that the use of other measures such as multi-factor authentication along with greater security awareness among CBPS employees may have prevented this data breach.

Victims were offered two years of free credit monitoring, but some chose to file class action suits. Even though CBPS's systems were directly breach and GE's own systems were not affected in the data breach, GE had to deal with the consequences.

Health Share of Oregon (2020) — Business Associate Data Breach

Health Share of Oregon is a consortium of local health care and insurance providers that provides coordinated care for health plan members in

Clackamas, Multnomah, and Washington counties. In January 2020, Health Share of Oregon notified 654,362 of their existing and former members that some of their protected health information (PHI) was stolen from its transportation contractor, GridWorks. The PHI exposed included names, addresses, contact telephone numbers, birth dates, Health Share ID numbers, Medicaid numbers, and Social Security numbers.

GridWorks informed that the information that was compromised was stored on a laptop and that the said laptop was stolen from the Portland office of GridWorks in a burglary in November 2019.

GridWorks was providing non-emergent medical transportation (Ride to Care) services to Health Share and in line with Health Care policies (and HIPAA guidelines) was bound as a business associate to use encryption on all portable devices. However, for reasons not made public, the data was not encrypted as required.

A similar data breach occurred when the Tuman Medical Center reported the theft of a laptop in December 2019 which impacted 114,466 patients. Such incidents have led to Business Associates being held accountable by the Department of Health and Human Services (HHSs) to protect PHI by following the three HIPAA rules (e.g., Security, Privacy, and Breach Notification Rules). HIPAA requires that entities and business associates implement a method to encrypt and decrypt electronic protected health information for all electronic PHI that is created, stored, or transmitted in systems and work devices such as a mobile phone, laptop, desktop, flash drive, hard drive).

In addition to notifying members of the breach, Health Share offered those affected a year of free credit monitoring, fraud consultation, and identity restoration services.

The SolarWinds Cyber-Attack (2020) — The Perfect Storm?

It is a hackers' dream to launch a cyber-attack that can impact many important organizations in one go by exploiting a single vulnerability that can inflict maximum damage. The SolarWinds cyber-attack, one of the most high-profile attacks in cyber history is an example of this. Hackers targeted SolarWinds a software company based in Tulsa, Okla., which provides system management tools for network and infrastructure monitoring. They figured that if they were to introduce malicious code into SolarWinds IT performance monitoring software (named Orion) they would enter thousands of organizations and government agencies around the world that used this software.

The hackers (allegedly backed by a nation state) planned and orchestrated a carefully planned attack that had several elements of a classic software supply chain attack. In general, software supply chain partners have access to organizational systems and in this case, Orion as an IT monitoring software had privileged access to IT systems to obtain log and system performance data. Hackers knew that this privileged position and its deployment across several thousand customers could help them cause damage on an unprecedented scale.

The hackers modus operandi was simple. They inserted malicious code into Orion software so that they could trigger attacks in enterprises and government agencies and other organizations who were clients of Orion software. Since the update was distributed by SolarWinds the update would get installed in targeted organizations without any suspicion.

As organizations around the world installed the update, the malware infected them. Prominent among the organizations affected were US government departments such as Homeland Security, State, Commerce, and Treasury as well as companies such as FireEye, Microsoft, Intel, Cisco, Nvidia, Belkin, and VMWare and Deloitte. While Orion had over 30,000 customers worldwide, it was reported that only 18,000 organizations installed malicious SolarWinds Orion code into their networks.

Every organization uses a variety of infrastructure, software, and systems supplied by third parties and such malicious exploitation of a simple update process was hitherto not experienced on such a massive scale. The news of this large-scale cyber-attack sent shock waves around the world, and what caused greater alarm was the way that third-party supplied software was leveraged. SolarWinds named the actual malicious code injection that was planted by hackers into Orion code as "Sunburst."

The SolarWinds breach has brought the issue of vulnerabilities via supply chain systems into sharp focus. Governments and Boards have started asking IT and Security managers as to how vulnerable their organizations are to such attacks and what steps can be taken to mitigate these risks. From understanding supply chain cyber vulnerabilities, evaluating software bill of materials (SBOMs) to relooking at vendor onboarding policies and processes to reviewing software updating processes and adopting zero trust approaches are all on the table. Going forward we can expect that greater priority will be accorded for implementing required security controls and actively managing security threats from supply chain systems as well as pressure on third-party vendors for better security monitoring and compliance.

Curiously, the purpose of the attack remains largely unknown, though many believe that it was a show of strength by a state backed hacker group. The attackers first gained access to the SolarWinds systems sometime in September 2019 and stayed undetected for several months until the hack was publicly reported until December 2020. As they had access for an extended period and could have caused greater damage (than reported), was this then just a test case for launching such supply chain attacks and a forerunner of more such attacks to come?

The phrase "perfect storm" was coined by author Sebastian Junger following a conversation with Meteorologist Robert Case where Case described the convergence of weather conditions as being "perfect" for the formation of such a storm. Have the hackers found that perfect combination of elements in the SolarWinds cyber-attack that could help them raise a cyber storm in future?

Instagram/Facebook/LinkedIn (2021) – An Unusual Case of a Breach at Two Levels

In January 2021, the popular social media giant Instagram suffered a data breach where personal information of millions of account holders was leaked. To start with a Chinese start-up SocialArks scraped the personal information of account holders from Instagram, Facebook, and LinkedIn and stored it in a database. Data scraping is the act of extracting users' private information from a website or social media platform without their consent or knowledge and in violation of the sites' data privacy policy.

The question arises if web scraping is an illegal act or is considered unethical if scraped contents are misused. There are many who consider it an unethical act, but there are also those who believe that any data scraped in disregard to the websites' terms of service, or its owner's permission could violate copyright law and contractual conditions.

SocialArks stored the scraped information on a cloud database. The database used was an opensource software called Elasticsearch and contained about 400 GB of public and private profiles. A cloud misconfiguration by SocialArks led to the exposure of 318 million records which included.[4]

Over 11 million Instagram user profiles, including names, phone numbers, usernames, profile pictures, email addresses, frequently used hashtags, and locations.

Over 82 million Facebook profiles consisting of information such as names, contact details, email addresses, Messenger IDs, Likes, and Facebook links to profile pictures, profile description, and pictures.

Sixty-six million LinkedIn user profiles containing names, email addresses, employment details, job profile connected social media account login names, etc.

This data breach was an unusual one. At one level, there was a data leak through scraping done by SocialArk, but at another level SocialArk was the "victim?" as the open-source database ElasticSearch was misconfigured. The data leak was discovered when the SocialArks server was found exposed to the Internet without even a username and password protection.

ElasticSearch is an open-source software that enables indexing and searching various kinds of data, such as indexed documents, personal data, customer sensitive information, etc. This ElasticSearch is known to have vulnerabilities and has been the target of several cyber-attacks.

While open-source products are developed with inputs from across the developer community and often provide great functionality, it must be remembered that they can be used entirely at the risk of organizations deploying them.

Kaseya (2021) – Another Supply Chain Nightmare

The American Independence Day Weekend in 2021 turned out to be a nightmare for Enterprise IT firm Kaseya. On July 3, they announced that they had become victims of a successful cyber-attack where hackers (allegedly the REvil/Sodinikibi ransomware group) carried out a supply chain ransomware attack by leveraging a vulnerability in Kaseya's VSA software which impacted their customers and Managed Service Providers (who used their software to provide remote monitoring and other administrative services).

While Kaseya had over 40,000 customers using their software, it was widely reported that an estimated 1,000 companies had their servers and workstations encrypted. Kaseya admitted that while a small number of Kaseya clients may have been directly infected, a larger number of small businesses further down the supply chain which depend on MSPs to provide services could have been impacted. Other sources who claimed to be close to the hackers indicated that more than a million systems could have been infected.

The hackers managed to circumvent authentication controls and used an authenticated session to upload the malicious payload, and then used a structured query language (SQL) injection for code execution. The attack exploited a zero-day vulnerability labeled CVE-2021-30116 and delivered the payload via a spurious update.

Kaseya's incident response team swung into action and proceeded to shut down its SaaS servers, notified customers of the breach, and advised their on-premises customers to shut off their VSA servers.

The hackers, meanwhile, made an offer to the victims that they would publish a universal decryptor which would enable them to recover their encrypted files in exchange for US$70 million payable in bitcoin.

Given the gravity of the cyber-attack and its potential consequences, FBI and CISA released advisories urging Kaseya's customers to implement multi-factor authentication as well as use a tool provided by the company to determine the risk of exploit.

Log4j (2021) – A Cyber Pandemic that Spreads through the Software Supply Chain

Having tasted success by attacking organizations through their supply chain partners and being able to cause greater damage across multiple targets could lead to hackers increasingly resort to launching more such attacks in the future.

Log4j is a popular logging framework/library (APIs) also known as an artifact in the Java ecosystem. It was developed by the Apache Software Foundation as a tracing or logging tool/API which is a common requirement for any large application. Over the years it has evolved further, gained wide acceptance among the developer community, and has been deployed in tens of thousands of software applications and projects. The Log4J framework is an open-source software licensed by the Apache Software Foundation.

Hackers discovered a flaw (known as log4shell) in Log4j logging tool which experts suggest could be the worst computer vulnerability discovered in years. The vulnerability was first reported to the Apache Software Foundation after it was discovered by a member of Alibaba's cloud security team in November 2021. It was potentially dangerous as it allowed arbitrary code execution which represents a nightmare scenario for security teams. It had existed since 2013 but was evidently overlooked. As logging is an important part of any application, it offered a way for hackers to introduce malicious code and cause damage without being noticed as logging being automated does not involve any human intervention.

The news of the vulnerability became public in December 2021 and set the alarm bells ringing as the logging tool is widely used across cloud servers and enterprise software as well as in industry and government sectors. If not fixed immediately, it would allow hackers easy access to internal networks where they could steal/erase valuable data and plant malware to launch further attacks.

While exact numbers of the impact are not available, estimates suggest that just for the Log4j-core over 17,000 packages might be affected. It was also found that 35,863 of the available artifacts which use Log4j may be affected.[5] While this data does not provide an indication of the number of organizations that could be affected, it suggests that potential damage could be widespread.

Another factor that makes assessment of the true impact complicated is the difficulty even at an organizational level to determine how many dependencies on log4j exist in their codes since there are many artifacts that depend on Log4j indirectly. This poses a challenge for organizations who want to install patches to fix the vulnerability at various levels of the dependency chain.

The Apache Software Foundation provided multiple patches starting in mid-December 2021 to address different vulnerabilities including new findings such as ways in which hackers could launch a denial of service (DOS) attack.

As organizations discover more dependencies on log4j within their systems and fix them, hackers continue to exploit associated vulnerabilities. The research team at Check Point Software Research calls it 'one of the most serious vulnerabilities on the internet in recent years.' To buttress their argument, they point to the fact that Apache Log4j is the most prevalent java logging library with over 400,000 downloads from its GitHub project and is used by many organizations worldwide. They further add that exploiting this vulnerability is relatively simple and allows hackers to gain control over Java-based web servers and launch remote code execution attacks.[6]

Colonial Pipeline Cyber-Attack (2021) – Shuts Down the Largest Fuel Pipeline in the United States

Darkside, a ransomware group compromised a third-party software vendor that provided remote access services to Colonial Pipeline. By exploiting a remote code execution vulnerability in PulseConnect Secure, a virtual private network (VPN) software program used by Colonial Pipeline, the attackers were able to monitor its pipeline operations. Once inside the Colonial Pipeline network, they encrypted its systems and demanded a ransom.

Colonial Pipeline was forced to shut down its oil for five days resulting in a gasoline shortage in the Southeastern United States. Colonial Pipeline succumbed to the ransom demand and paid a ransom of US$4.4 million to the attackers to regain access to its systems.

GitHub (2022) – Breach Exposes Private Repositories of Dozens of Organizations

GitHub (owned by Microsoft) is the world's leading AI-powered developer platform. In April 2022, threat actors used stolen user tokens from Heroku and TravisCI to gain access to private repositories hosted by GitHub. Heroku is a container-based cloud Platform as a Service (PaaS) which developers use to deploy, manage, and scale contemporary apps while Travis CI is a continuous integration and deployment platform. They exploited an unknown vulnerability in OAuth tokens which GitHub had adopted recently. Media reports suggest that more than 4,000 GitHub repositories could be impacted.[7]

Airbus (2023) – Data Leak of 3,200 Vendors via Partner Airline's Account

Airbus the European aerospace giant became a victim of a data breach that exposed confidential business information of over 3,200 Airbus vendors. The attackers called themselves "USDoD" gained access through a compromised account of Turkish Airlines employee account using the Redline info-stealer malware and used it to access Airbus web portal. The incident once again highlighted the vulnerability of companies to supply chain attacks, where threat actors target a weaker link in their network of suppliers, vendors, or third-party software libraries. Investigations revealed that an attempt to download an unauthorized version of the Microsoft.NET framework was responsible for the infection, which resulted in the installation of info-stealing software on the employee's computer.[8]

Norton (2023) – Norton Antivirus Users Hit by Malicious Software Update

Norton is today a brand owned by Gen Digital who also owns other security software brands such as Avast, LifeLock, Avira, AVG, ReputationDefender and CCleaner. Norton is best known for its widely used antivirus software. In May 2023, they were also affected by a supply chain attack. Attackers exploited a zero-day vulnerability in MOVEit Transfer, a managed file transfer software that was used by Norton's parent company, Gen Digital to transfer files between its offices and customers.

Microsoft (2023) – Microsoft Falls Victim Supply Chain Attack via Jfrog Artifactory

It is no secret that Microsoft Windows has the dominant share of the Operating Systems (OS) market. For hackers Microsoft products and services are a hot target – a fact that Microsoft is aware of. The company works diligently on known vulnerabilities and to mitigate impact of cyber-attacks. In February 2023, attackers exploited a vulnerability in Jfrog Artifactory, a binary repository manager that Microsoft uses to store and distribute its software components.

By gaining access to Jfrog Artifactory, Diamond Sleet a group of hackers injected malicious code into some of Microsoft's software components enabling them to steal source code and other confidential information.

Once again in October 2023, North Korean threat actors Diamond Sleet and Onyx Sleet got together and exploited a vulnerability in the Jet Brains TeamCity software development and integration platform. The vulnerability, CVE-2023-42793, permitted remote code execution on the TeamCity server and its agents. This time the hackers exploited this vulnerability compromise the TeamCity instances of several organizations, including Microsoft. They inserted malicious code into the software build and delivery processes thereby severely impacting Microsoft customers.

Protection from Supply Chain Attacks

Even as organizations recognize and implement security measures, supply chain cyber-attacks continue to pose a serious and rising threat to security and integrity of software and systems of organizations of all sizes and sectors.

Threats from software supply chain partners are today one of the most potent of all threats. Attackers have become adept at exploiting the trust and dependencies that exist between software suppliers and their customers which can potentially result in having devastating consequences for both. Four key lessons that we can learn from software supply chain attacks are as follows:

- The need to be aware of the risks and vulnerabilities of the software supply chain. For example, the maintenance of SBOMs to document and track the components and dependencies of application software including verification of their integrity and authenticity. It is important to note that on May 12, 2021, President Biden's Executive Order on Improving the Nation's Cybersecurity was issued, emphasizing, for the first time, the need to enhance software supply chain security.
- The need to use tools and techniques such as code signing, checksums, and digital signatures verify the source and integrity of our software updates and patches.
- Use frameworks and protocols such as the Software Supply Chain Integrity Framework and the Software Component Transparency protocol to communicate and collaborate with suppliers and customers.
- Adopt a defense-in-depth approach to software security, whereby there is no reliance on a single layer or vendor for protection.

Further to mitigate the risk from other types of supply chain attacks a collaborative and coordinated effort from both the buyers and their suppliers is required. Important steps that must be taken by organizations in this regard are:

- Onboard supply chain partners after conducting due diligence on third parties before engaging them and monitor their performance and compliance regularly.
- Enhance visibility into systems and networks of supply chain participants.
- Execute contractual agreements that define security controls and related compliance requirements and the roles and responsibilities of each party for data protection and incident response.
- Implement encryption, authentication, backup, and other security measures to protect data in transit and at rest when sharing it with third parties.
- Educate and enhance awareness among employees and customers on how to recognize and avoid phishing emails and other social engineering attacks that may compromise their credentials or devices.
- Perform regular audits to ensure that supply chain participants comply with security standards and best practices.

Notes

1   Jones, C. (2022, May 3). Warnings (& lessons) of the 2013 target data breach. Red River|Technology decisions aren't black and white. Think Red. https://redriver.com/security/target-data-breach.
2   Smith, M. (2014, November 10). Home Depot IT: Get hacked, blame Windows, switch execs to MacBooks. *Network World*. Retrieved from https://www.giac.org/paper/gsec/36253/case-study-home-depot-data-breach/143349.
3   Winter, M. (2014, November 7). Home Depot hackers used vendor log-on to steal data, e-mails. Retrieved from http://www.usatoday.com/story/money/business/2014/11/06/home-depot-hackers-stolen-data/18613167.
4   Team, S. C., & Team, S. C. (2021, May 7). Chinese start-up leaked 400GB of scraped data exposing 200+ million Facebook, Instagram, and LinkedIn users. SafetyDetectives. https://www.safetydetectives.com/blog/socialarks-leak-report/.
5   Google (2021, December 17). Understanding the impact of Apache Log4J vulnerability. *Google Online Security Blog*. https://security.googleblog.com/2021/12/understanding-impact-of-apache-log4j.html.
6   Bferrite, & Bferrite. (2021, December 23). Apache Log4J vulnerability - Check point blog. *Check Point Blog*. https://blog.checkpoint.com/security/protecting-against-cve-2021-44228-apache-log4j2-versions-2-14-1/.

7   Staff, S. (2023, September 13). Repojacking attack could impact thousands of GitHub repositories. *SC Media*. https://www.scmagazine.com/brief/repojacking-attack-could-impact-thousands-of-github-repositories.

8   Baran, G. (2023, September 12). Airbus Cyber attack: Over 3,200 vendor data accessed by hackers. *Cyber Security News*. https://cybersecuritynews.com/airbus-cyber-attack/.

4

CHALLENGES IN VENDOR CYBER RISK MANAGEMENT

Vendor Inventory

Companies must document the vendors they have and how they may cause cyber risk. There are four different types of vendors related to cybersecurity: system vendors, technology vendors, CSP vendors, and service provider vendors.

What type of cyber risk do you have with a CSP? The #1 risk is a data breach. Companies are responsible for notifying their employees, customers, partners, and the like of a data breach, NOT the CSP. If your contract says otherwise, we suggest revising it. You do not want your most valuable relationships in the hands of anyone but you.

If the CSP has software that is being used as a critical service, you also need to understand your business interruption risk related to service level agreements (SLAs) with the receiver of the critical service.

What type of cyber risk do you have with a system provider? The #1 risk for this type of vendor is malware in patches. As we have seen with

DOI: 10.4324/9781003581321-5

the SolarWinds disaster, malware in patches provides an open door to the attackers.

What type of cyber risk do you have with a technology provider? Same as with the system provider: malware in patches.

What type of cyber risk do you have with a service provider? The #1 risk for this type of vendor is that the contractors have malicious intent to steal your data, disrupt your business, or do physical harm to your employees.

How do you get a vendor inventory? There are several ways to do this.

1. Interview your staff. This is time-consuming, tedious, and not a happy project for your company. It also costs a lot of money. OR
2. Scan the infrastructure for identification of system, technology, and cloud service vendors. This is inexpensive, accurate, quick, and completely automated. This is the most effective solution.

   The scan should identify all of the assets in the client's environment regardless of what technology they are deployed on. Discover all the network and subnet devices including routers, servers, switches, etc. This discovery includes all the metadata about those devices such as manufacturer, version, IP address, etc. Other scans should discover all the hardware including manufacturer, version, IP address, etc., and all the software. This includes business applications and infrastructure applications. Infrastructure applications include your cybersecurity tool stack. Metadata collected includes patch levels, manufacturers, record counts, etc. The end result is a digital asset inventory of the entire infrastructure where technology, system, and cloud service vendors can be identified.

   Further scans provide cybersecurity tool and control effectiveness. These readiness scans show where the gaps are in the coverage of tools and controls. These scans include:
   - Database Security
   - Cloud Security
   - Permissioning
   - File Security
   - Endpoint
   - Patch Management
   - Firewall Security
   - User Security

Table 4.1 Vendor Financial Impacts

Vendor	Data Breach Impact	Ransomware	DDoS	Regulatory
A	$4,000,000	$ –	$ –	$2,500,000
B	$3,000,000	$ –	$ –	$ –
B	$1,000,000	$ –	$ –	$ –

3. Get copies of all your contracts and SOWs. If you have a procurement team that keeps good records, this is a start. Drawbacks include having to sort through thousands of documents to get the data you want.

Vendor Assessment Prioritization and Due Diligence

Prioritization of the vendor assessments should be objective and allow the company to focus on the high-risk vendors first. Using red, amber, and green types of analysis is subjective and not useful.

Quantifying potential data loss, ransomware loss, DDoS loss, and regulatory losses provide a complete picture of how important each vendor is to your business (Table 4.1).

Another common challenge of third-party risk management (TPRM) implementation is determining what risk assessment activities are necessary to audit a vendor's risk profile successfully.[1] While performing due diligence, an organization can assign vendors based on risk types.

Risk types allow organizations to manage and accurately assess the level of risk a vendor presents to the organization. Organizations that don't incorporate risk types into their due diligence plan will have difficulty determining if a particular vendor is safe to do business with. Organizations with many third-party partnerships will also struggle to prioritize high-risk vendors.

Vendor Security Questionnaire vs. IT Asset Scanner

Vendor security questionnaires are rubbish. Self-reporting does not work. Answers are biased and incentive focused. Additionally, dispatching security questionnaires across your supply chain, ensuring each vendor completes the questionnaire on time, and verifying the validity of each vendor's answers is a significant challenge for any organization.

The answer to the security questionnaire is to use automated scanning software to answer these questions and allow for a self-service portal to upload evidence to support information that needs to be provided manually.

IT Asset Scanners can provide a view of cybersecurity readiness. Gaps are identified based upon the coverage of the cybersecurity tools. It demonstrates gaps such as:

- Endpoint – How many endpoints don't have EDR in place?
- Antivirus – Where is antivirus missing?
- End of Life (EOL) – Which systems and technologies are EOL?
- Password Compliance Management – Which users are not compliant with HIPAA, NYSDFS, FDIC, etc.?
- Patch Management – What version of the software should be applied and what version of the software is in place?
- Database Security – Where is there unmapped PII? Where is native encryption not in place?
- MFA – Which users are not using MFA?

Determining Risk Related to Vendors

A complete vendor-risk management software will allow an organization to:

- Proactively detect third-party security risks.
- Rank security risks by severity.
- Request remediation from vendors.
- Waive non-critical risks.
- Gather security evidence, and
- Prioritize remediation across their entire supply chain.

It's important to note that high-risk vendors will likely require more intensive TPRM strategies. An organization's highest-risk vendors will likely require remote or onsite audits to ensure information security. In contrast, low-risk vendors may only need regulatory compliance checks to confirm low operational risk.[2]

Financial cyber risk metrics should include:

- Financial exposures for data loss
- Financial exposures for ransomware loss

- Financial exposures for DDoS loss
- Financial exposures for regulatory loss
- Technology Risk – where you should diversify your risk, Cloud, IoT, IA, etc.
- Regulatory financial risk – what systems are in scope for GDPR, CCPA, how much financial exposure they have, how do you reduce the financial exposures.

Continuous Control Monitoring

Commonly used assessment methods which are a part of an organization's TPRM process only evaluate a vendor at that current moment. This can open an organization to hidden security risks as assessment data becomes outdated and a vendor's security posture changes.

It is important to maintain an updated view of an individual vendor's risk exposure on an ongoing basis. For this an organization should implement continuous monitoring processes into its TPRM program. Continuous monitoring is the process of passively monitoring cybersecurity tools and controls throughout the lifecycle of a third-party relationship.

Benefits of continuous monitoring include:

- Significantly increase incident response metrics.
- Improve ongoing visibility across all the vendors.
- Eliminate blind spots that can occur in between evaluation cycles.
- Provide security control and tool updates in real-time.

Automation

As an organization grows, the number of third-party partnerships increases at a higher ratio. This makes the TPRM program more challenging to maintain. Implementing automation is the best way for a business to get objective data, reduce costs, and put the work into the hands of the third party.

Automation makes processes more standard, risks easier to identify, mitigation more transparent, and new vendors easier to onboard. Automated solutions will also integrate with regulatory compliance, and continuous monitoring.

Additional benefits of having an automated TPRM program include:

- Eliminating the need for manual tasks and tedious data entry
- Improving business continuity by streamlining TPRM procedures
- Passively enforcing regulatory requirements
- Improving risk-based decision-making by increasing visibility
- Anticipating security breaches and overall strengthening of TPRM procedures

Notes

1   8 Third-Party risk management Challenges + Solutions and Tips|UpGuard (n.d.). https://www.upguard.com/blog/tprm-challenges.
2   8 Third-Party risk management Challenges + Solutions and Tips|UpGuard (n.d.). https://www.upguard.com/blog/tprm-challenges.

PART II

VENDOR CYBER RISK MANAGEMENT – REGULATIONS AND COMPLIANCE

5

VENDOR CYBERSECURITY REGULATIONS

Regulations Requiring Vendor Cyber Risk Programs

The PCI Security Council

The PCI Security Council (PCI SC) was formed in 2004 by the major card brands, including American Express, JBC, Visa, Mastercard, and Discover to protect cardholder data. It applies to merchants, acquiring banks, and data processors. Data processors are typically third parties, however each of these three has first and third-party relationships.

The PCI SC is one of the earliest governing bodies to have vendor cybersecurity requirements. They require all payment card service providers who process, transmit, and/or store payment card information to be compliant with the Payment Card Industry Data Security Standard (PCI-DSS).

Vendors must submit an Attestation of Compliance every 12 months. An attestation is completed by a Qualified Security Assessor and states that the

DOI: 10.4324/9781003581321-7

organization is PCI DSS compliant. It is used as evidence that an organization has upheld security best practices to protect cardholder data. Each vendor submits an AOC as a service provider.

Each vendor must submit a quarterly Approved Scanning Vendor (ASV) report and the current years' penetration test of the external network. No vulnerabilities should exist that are scored 4.0 or higher by the CVSS in the Quarterly ASV scan report. The PCI Compliance team will only accept a maximum of three versions of an AOC from the same vendor for review in a 12-month period. The PCI Compliance team may request that the vendor provide a demo on their payment processing workflow through its services.

Third-party service providers can store, process, or transmit cardholder data on behalf of the first party. They may also manage systems or technologies that store or process cardholder data. These may include payment systems, routers, firewalls, databases, physical security, and/or servers.

The use of a third party does not exclude the first party's responsibility to ensure that its cardholder data environment is secure. Clear policies and procedures must be part of the vendor risk management program. These must outline all applicable security requirements; ownership and auditing of those measures must be reported on regularly.

Proper due diligence and cyber risk analysis are critical components in the selection of any third-party vendor. Requirements from the PCI SC include four major components[1] when selecting vendors – proper due diligence, service correlation, a written cyber program, and monitoring of the third parties.

PCI requires Third-Party Service Provider (TPSP) Due Diligence for vendors that process or store cardholder data.[2] Vendors must be put through a rigorous vetting process using careful due diligence prior to the establishment of the relationship.

PCI requires Service Correlation to the PCI DSS Requirements for TPSPs. This includes understanding how the services provided by TPSPs correspond to the applicable PCI DSS requirements.

PCI requires Written Agreements and Policies and Procedures for TPSPs. Detailed written agreements will ensure mutual understanding between the organization and its TPSP(s) concerning their respective responsibilities and obligations with respect to PCI DSS compliance requirements. PCI requires the firm to monitor TPSP Compliance Status.

National Association of Insurance Commissioners (NAIC)[3]

The NAIC – Insurance Data Security Act (also known as the Model Law) requires oversight of TPSP Arrangements. A Licensee (person, broker, carrier, reinsurance firms that are required to be licensed, authorized, or registered pursuant to the insurance laws of this state) shall exercise due diligence in selecting its TPSP; and require the TPSP to implement the necessary administrative, technical, and physical safeguards to protect and secure the Information Systems and Nonpublic Information they have access to.

The TPRM program must have a formal process in place whereby:[4]

1. Risk is assessed based on the company's understanding of the third-party service provider's information security program as well as by the company's ability to verify elements of the third-party service provider's security program.
2. Based on the company's risk, the company ranks vendors and uses a vendor ranking to determine the depth and frequency of review procedures performed related to ongoing vendor relationships.
3. The company determines appropriate access rights based on the risk assessment and company business needs.
4. The company designs specific mitigation strategies, including network monitoring specific to third-party service providers and access controls, where appropriate.

If the Licensee suspects that a cybersecurity incident has occurred in a system maintained by a TPSP, the Licensee will perform a forensics investigation. During the investigation it must be determined whether a Cybersecurity Incident has occurred. The nature and scope of the Cybersecurity Incident must be documented and any Nonpublic Information (NPI) that may have been involved in the Cybersecurity Incident identified. The firm must ensure that they restore the security of the Information Systems compromised in the Cybersecurity Event.

In the case of a cybersecurity incident, notification has to be provided in electronic form as directed by the Commissioner. Required information includes:

- Date of the occurrence of the Cybersecurity Incident.
- A description of how the information was compromised, including the specific roles and responsibilities of TPSPs, if any.
- How the Cybersecurity Incident was identified.
- If any lost, stolen, or breached information has been recovered and if so, how this was done.
- Who discovered the Cybersecurity Incident.
- Whether a police report or other regulatory, government or law enforcement agencies are notified and, if so, when such notification was provided.

Third-party service providers must notify their affected Insurers and the Commissioner of Insurance in the state in which they are domiciled within 72 hours of a Cybersecurity Incident involving NPI that they are processing or storing on behalf of a Licensee.

Notification is also required to producers of record of all affected Consumers as soon as practicable as directed by the Commissioner if there is a Cybersecurity Incident involving NPI that is being processed or stored by its TPSP.

European Union — GDPR

Article 28 of the GDPR states that — If an organization uses one or more third parties to process personal info ("processors") it must ensure they are also compliant with GDPR.[5]

This requires a leader to oversee the vendor cyber risk management program and to put in place the program requirements that are needed.

Vendor relationship management processes and procedures must ensure that third parties that process personal information (PI) are compliant with the GDPR. This can also be a role of the Data Protection Officer (DPO) if there is no vendor management team. The DPO Job Responsibilities and the Rationale for a Data Protection Officer (DPO) are required.

State of CA — California Consumer Protection Act (CCPA)[6]

With respect to third-party risk, the CCPA recognizes, and places obligations on, service providers. These are defined as entities that process consumers' PI on the business's behalf and third parties are defined as entities to whom the business shares or sells PI but do not directly collect PI from consumers. In particular, the CCPA emphasizes contractual requirements and the consumer's right to opt-out of the sale of PI.

For service providers, businesses must maintain records of each service provider and the categories of PI disclosed to them. The organization must conduct due diligence with potential service providers prior to entering into a contract. The contracts must be re-evaluated on at least an annual basis. The company must have a written contract with the service providers that prohibits them from retaining, using, or disclosing the PI for any purpose other than for the exact purposes of performing the services agreed to in the contract, or as otherwise permitted by the CCPA. There must be language in the contract to help cure a violation of the CCPA. The service provider must notify the company without unreasonable delay upon experiencing a data breach. The contract must require the service provider to protect the PI disclosed to it by developing and maintaining reasonable security safeguards appropriate to the information.

In terms of Consumer Rights, the contract must require the service provider to delete a consumer's PI when you direct it to do so and obligate the service provider to assist you in complying with a consumer's request to know / to disclose the PI collected, shared, or sold.

There must be processes in place that enable the company to notify a service provider when consumers exercise a right.

All categories of data that a third-party touch must be documented and the business purpose of the data exchange with each third party must be clearly stated. Records must be maintained of third-party data exchanges in the preceding 12 months, including the categories of PI.

The third-party must have accurate records of the data exchanges so that you can disclose to consumers the categories of PI sold and the categories of third parties to whom you have sold that PI. They must provide confirmation that your firm gave a consumer proper notice and the right to opt out, and a signed attestation describing the notice, along with an example of the notice. They must have processes in place that guarantee the accuracy of the attestation. They must be able to cease selling a consumer's PI no later than 15 days after receipt of the consumer's request to opt out of the sale of their PI.

Upon the receipt of a consumer's request to opt out of the sale of PI, they must have processes in place to notify a third party of the consumer's request and to instruct the third party not to further sell that consumer's PI. They must maintain records of parties to whom they have sold a consumer's PI within 90 days prior to the consumer's opt-out request.

New York State Department of Financial Services – NYCRR Part 500

Each Covered Entity (person operating under or required to operate under a license, registration, charter, certificate, permit, accreditation, or similar authorization under the Banking Law, the Insurance Law, or the Financial Services Law) must implement a set of written policies and procedures that are designed to safeguard the security of Information Systems and NPI that are processed or stored by a TPSP.

Requirements include that:

- these policies and procedures must be based on a Risk Assessment of the Covered Entity and identify all TPSPs and access their cybersecurity practices to ensure that they met by such TPSPs in order for them to do business with the Covered Entity.
- a rigorous due diligence is done to evaluate the adequacy of cybersecurity practices of such TPSPs.
- periodic assessment of such TPSPs based on the risk they present and the continued adequacy of their cybersecurity practices.
- the policies and procedures shall include relevant guidelines for due diligence and/or contractual protections relating to TPSPs including to the extent applicable guidelines addressing.
- the TPSP's policies and procedures for access controls.
- the use of Multi-Factor Authentication as required by section 500.12.
- the TPSP's policies and procedures for use of encryption as required by section 500.15 to protect NPI in transit and at rest.
- a notification process must be in place to the Covered Entity in the event of a Cybersecurity Incident directly impacting the Covered Entity's

Information Systems or the Covered Entity's NPI that is processes or stored by the TPSP.

All the TPRM programs start with a vendor inventory. Not only who they are but what type of vendor they are. Vendors can have more than one function. As an example, Salesforce is both a cloud service and a system vendor. It is not enough to have a list of applications that are vendor supported. You must know the vendor and what they provide you.

A vendor's risk assessment must look at what is important. How much data exfiltration, business interruption, and regulatory risk do you have with the vendor?

Security Assessment. How effective are the vendor's cybersecurity controls? A NIST or ISO assessment should be reviewed in depth. Security issues should be prioritized to fix.

Vendor background checks and due diligence require more than a useless SOC 2 report.

Language about how data breaches will be managed in detail with a communications and incident response plan is required.

Procedures should include guidelines for due diligence and contractual protection.

All third parties should connect using multi-factor authentication.

Non-public information should be encrypted in transit and at rest for cloud service providers that have sensitive data on their network.

Security incidents must be communicated by the third party to your firm within a specific timeframe. It is recommended to put in the contractual protections that in the event of a breach, they have 72 hours to report it to you. If they do not notify you and the breach is made public, the examiners are going to come after you and ask why it was not reported to them within 72 hours. All 50 states have data breach notification laws.

There are many issues with contracts. In one instance, I recall where the vendor told a company- "if there's a breach, that is not our fault, we expect to still get paid regardless and we accept no responsibility." And the company signed it. When I saw the contract, I said, you know, you made a mistake, right? They had to revisit the contract and put the right language in because it was not reviewed properly. This had to go back to the business that engaged the vendor. The big issues with vendor management today are that the business selects the vendor and cyber is not involved. This must change. This should be baked into a policy that allows for this issue to no longer exist.

Department of Defense — CMMC

The Department of Defense (DoD) created a new program called the Cybersecurity Maturity Model Certification (CMMC). The DoD is requiring all contractors who manage sensitive DoD data to have a third-party maturity assessment in order to obtain DoD business. This requirement is effective July 1, 2020.

The Office of the Under Secretary of Defense for Acquisition and Sustainment (OUSD (A&S)) recognizes that security is foundational to acquisition and should not be traded along with cost, schedule, and performance moving forward. The Department is committed to working with the Defense Industrial Base (DIB) sector to enhance the protection of CUI within the supply chain.

OUSD (A&S) is working with DoD stakeholders, University Affiliated Research Centers (UARCs), Federally Funded Research and Development Centers (FFRDC), and industry to develop the Cybersecurity Maturity Model Certification (CMMC).

The CMMC is a cybersecurity audit that measures the cybersecurity maturity levels of a company. Results from the Audit can range from "Basic Cybersecurity Hygiene" to "Advanced/Progressive." The intent of the DoD is to incorporate CMMC into Defense Federal Acquisition Regulation Supplement (DFARS) and use it as a requirement for contract awards.

CMMC Levels 1–3 have 110 security requirements which are specified in NIST SP 800-171 rev1. CMMC incorporates additional practices and processes from other standards, references, and sources materials. These include the NIST SP 800-53, the Aerospace Industries Association (AIA) National Aerospace Standard (NAS) 9933 "Critical Security Controls for Effective Capability in Cyber Defense," and the Computer Emergency Response Team (CERT) Resilience Management Model (RMM) v1.2.

The CMMC will review and combine various cybersecurity standards, best practices, and map these controls and processes across several maturity levels that range from basic cyber hygiene to advanced. For a given CMMC level, the associated controls, and processes, when implemented, will reduce risk against a specific set of cyber threats.

The CMMC effort builds upon existing regulation (DFARS 252.204-7012) that is based on trust by adding a verification component with respect to cybersecurity requirements.

The goal is for CMMC to be cost-effective and affordable for small businesses to implement at the lower CMMC levels. The intent is for certified independent third-party organizations to conduct audits and inform the DoD about vendor cyber risk.

Health and Human Services HIPAA and HiTech Acts[7]

Business Associates are third parties that are regulated by HIPAA. They are defined by HHS as any individual or organization that creates, receives, maintains, or transmits PHI on behalf of a Covered Entity (CE). It defines subcontractors as those that create, receive, maintain, or transmit PHI on behalf of a Business Associate.

For healthcare providers that are considered Covered Entities your responsibilities include that you ensure that all your vendors who manage PHI and are designated as Business Associates under HIPAA, and their subcontractors are compliant.

Twenty percent of all PHI breaches are caused by a Business Associate. If a Business Associates or their Subcontractors gets audited, so will the Covered Entity. Business associates include administration, data processors, accountants, management consultants, IT system, and service providers, document disposal companies, EHR/EMR providers, leasing companies, call centers, document management services, lawyers, claim processors, technology vendors, financial services, data centers, telco vendors, cloud service providers, medical billers, and collection agencies, among others.

Vendors must follow the HIPAA Security Rule (2005) for electronic Protected Health Information (ePHI). This includes:

1. Administrative Safeguards – Includes security management processes, workforce security, information access management, security training and awareness, contingency plan evaluation, and Business Associate contract.
2. Physical Safeguards – Includes facility access controls, workstation use, workstation security, and device and media control.

3. Technical Safeguards – Includes access control, audit control, integrity, personal, or entity authentication and transmission security.

The HITECH Act of 2009 (Health Information Technology for Economic and Clinical Health Act) applies to Business Associates. It extended the privacy and security rules of HIPAA to Businesses Associates and their subcontractors.

The HITECH Act was enacted to promote the adoption of health information technology, named EHR (electronic health records). HITECH gives health providers technical requirements to hospitals and doctors who are using EHR. After 2009, this Act requires Business Associates to implement the same compliance documents and training as a Covered Entity.

The Omnibus Rule (2013)

Under the Omnibus Rule, Business Associates are independently responsible to comply with HIPAA privacy, security and breach rule and are subject to fines.

First-party responsibilities with Business Associates include:

Having an up-to-date Business Associate Agreement (BAA) with each business associate that is reviewed and updated every year. The agreement must confirm what data the Business Associate uses that is PHI, why the Business Associate (BA) was engaged and how they will safeguard the PHI from misuse. The agreement governs the BA's creation, use, maintenance, and disclosure of PHI. The BA must comply with HIPAA Security and help a Covered Entity (CE) satisfy privacy rules and treat subcontractors as Business Associates. Business Associates are liable for the following:

*   use that is not permissible.
*   disclosures.
*   failures to provide breach notification to the CE.
*   failure to provide a copy of the ePHI to either the CE, the individual, or the individual's designee.
*   failure to follow minimum necessary standards when using or disclosing and failure to provide an accounting of disclosures.

Business associates that do not comply with HIPAA are liable for Civil Penalties. These penalties are mandatory for willful neglect. The HHSs Office for Civil Rights ("OCR") is responsible for enforcing the Privacy and Security Rule for HPAA Covered Entities.[8] OCR is required to impose HIPAA penalties if the Business Associate acted with willful neglect. This means that the Business Associate consciously, and intentionally failed to comply or showed reckless indifference to the obligation to comply with the HIPAA requirements.

A single action most often results in multiple violations. The loss of a record is a violation. As an example, the loss of a laptop containing records of five hundred individuals is a loss of five hundred records. This means in HIPAA language that there are five hundred violations.

If there was a failure to implement the required policies and safeguards, each day the Covered Entity failed to have the required policy or safeguard in place constitutes a separate violation. HIPAA penalties add up quickly. The OCR has imposed millions of dollars in penalties and settlements over the past several years. Additionally, State Attorneys General have the authority to sue for HIPAA violations and recover penalties of US$25,000 per violation plus attorneys' fees. The following chart summarizes the tiered penalty structure (Figure 5.1).

HIPAA Violation Penalty Tiers

First Tier	Second Tier
The covered entity did not know and could not reasonably have known about the breach. $120-$60,226 per violation	The covered entity knew or by exercising reasonable diligence, would have known of the violation; they did not act with willful neglect and could not reasonably have known about the breach. $1,205-$60,226 per violation
Third Tier	**Fourth Tier**
The covered entity acted with willful neglect and corrected the problem within 30 days. $12,045-$60,226 per violation	The covered entity acted with willful neglect and failed to make a timely correction. $60,226-$1,806,757 per violation

Figure 5.1 HIPAA Fines

Source: US Government Publishing Office. (2009, October 1). Content details 45 CFR 160.404. Amount of a civil money penalty. https://www.govinfo.gov/app/details/CFR-2009-title45-vol1/CFR-2009-title45-vol1-sec160-404.

HIPAA has the longest and one of the costliest penalties and settlements history in the United States. A single cyber event mostly likely results in multiple violations.[9] HIPAA considers willful neglect when imposing penalties. If the Business Associate did not act with willful neglect, the OCR may waive or reduce the penalties, depending on the circumstances. Willful negligence is indicated when the conduct is deliberate. Willful negligence involves behavior that is intended, and reckless.[10]

When the Business Associate was not willfully negligent and corrects the violation within 30 days, the OCR may choose not to impose any penalty. Having a plan and showing that changes were made to remediate the issue are key here. This is why having a cybersecurity program with policies and procedures that provides the requirements for the technical, physical, and administrative safeguards may protect the Business Associate from an extremely high penalty.

Furthermore, HIPAA violations may be a crime. Clinicians, healthcare staff members, data processors, insurance companies among others have been prosecuted for improperly accessing, using, or disclosing PHI. The maximum criminal penalties under HIPAA include jail time of one year to ten years, and fines from US$250 to US$50,000.[11]

In a Memorandum of Opinion released in 2005, the Department of Justice (DOJ) made a point of differentiating intent and knowledge. They define "knowingly" as referring to knowledge of the facts that comprise the offense and not the knowledge of the law being violated.[12]

Federal law prohibits any person from improperly obtaining or revealing PHI from a Covered Entity without authorization. Violations may result in the following criminal penalties (Figure 5.2).

Business Associates must report HIPAA breaches of unsecured PHI to Covered Entities that are affected. The Covered Entities must then notify affected individual(s) of the breach and to HHS. The Covered Entity will have to incur the data exfiltration costs associated with the data breach, the costs of responding to the HHS investigation, and the potential penalties. Not reporting opens both the Business Associate and the Covered Entity to civil penalties and opens the firm up to civil lawsuits.

The privacy rules of HIPAA are remarkably like GDPR. The Covered Entities and their Business Associates may not collect, use, or disclose PHI without the person's valid HIPAA authorization.

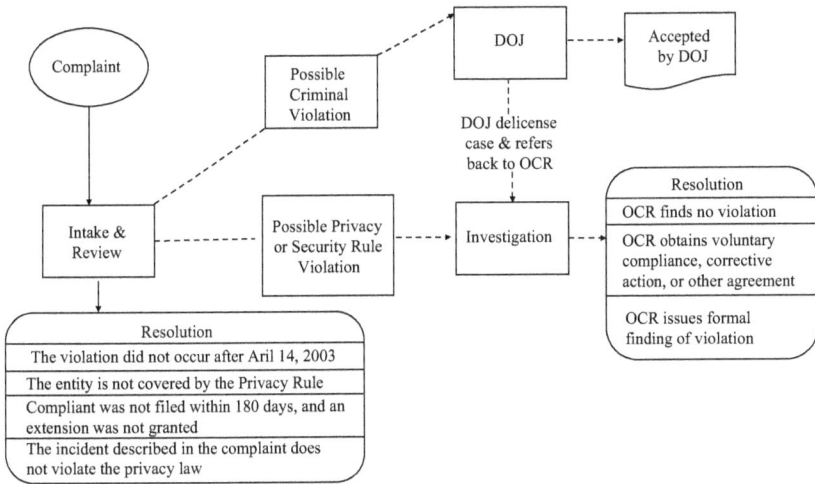

Figure 5.2 HIPAA Privacy & Security Rule Complaint Process
Source: US Department of Justice. (2022). https://hhs.gov/hipaa/for-professionals/compliance-enforcement/enforcement-process/index.html.

The Business Associate needs to have a cybersecurity risk analysis performed and the Covered Entity must ensure they have adequate security safeguards in place.

State of CO – Colorado Consumer Protection Act[13]

Colorado defines a third-party service provider as an entity that has been contracted to process or store PI on behalf of a Covered Entity.

A new requirement to ensure protections are in place when PII is transferred to third-party service providers.

Colorado requires that the third-party service provider implement and maintain reasonable security procedures and practices appropriate to the personal identifying information processes or stored by the third-party service provider. They must use safeguards that are designed to protect personal identifying information from unauthorized access, use, modification, disclosure, or destruction.

The Bill also was amended to include an exception where Covered Entity retains security responsibility and implements controls to protect PII from unauthorized disclosure or to eliminate third-party's access:

... disclosure of personal identifying information does not include disclosure of information to a third-party under circumstances where the covered entity retains primary responsibility for implementing and maintaining reasonable security procedures and practices appropriate to the nature of the personal identifying information and the covered entity implements and maintains technical controls that are reasonably designed to:

a.   help protect the personal identifying information from unauthorized access, use, modification, disclosure, or destruction; or
b.   effectively eliminate the third-party's ability to access the personal identifying information, notwithstanding the third-party's physical possession of the personal identifying information.

At the state level, Colorado now has the highest cost per record fine in the country as of this writing – a whopping US$20,000 a record.

Federal Trade Commission (FTC) – Graham-Leach-Bliley Act (GLBA)[14]

Companies in scope for GLBA are financial institutions, and those firms that offer financial products and services to individuals. These include loans, financial advice, investment advice or insurance.

GLBA defines Nonpublic Personal Information (NPI) as all data that is Personally Identifiable Information (PII) and financial information that is provided by a customer to the financial institution which results in a transaction with the customer.

Data that is public but has been made private (e.g., private emails, unlisted phone numbers, etc.), must be treated as nonpublic. GLBA definitions of NPI include an individual's income, social security number, marital status, amount of savings or investments, payment history, loan or deposit balance, credit or debit card purchases, account numbers, or consumer reports.

The Safeguards Rule requires financial institutions to create, implement, and maintain an all-inclusive cybersecurity plan which outlines the administrative, technical, and physical safeguards that are appropriate organization based on its size, complexity, and its financial activities. Safeguards should:

- Ensure the confidentiality, integrity, and availability of all NPI.
- Protect against the most common cyber threats.
- Protect against data breaches, and unauthorized access to NPI.

The cybersecurity plan must include:

- At least one employee who is responsible for the information security program and its safeguards.
- Have a risk management program that includes internal risks, third-party risks and fourth-party risks to the confidentiality, integrity, and availability of NPI.
- Perform a rigorous cybersecurity risk assessment which assesses the effectiveness of the cybersecurity safeguards in place to mitigate all risk types.
- Regular testing of cybersecurity controls, systems, and procedures.

The Safeguards Rule forces financial institutions to take cyber risk management seriously by measuring their cybersecurity risk and the effectiveness of their controls, systems, and procedures to reduce that risk to acceptable levels.

Summary

Each vendor-related regulation requires an understanding of the regulatory scope, cybersecurity programs and the use of cybersecurity control framework in the vendor management and assessment processes. In Chapter 11, we provided an understanding of the controls across different frameworks. All frameworks aspire to provide a level of control effectiveness relative to administrative, technical, and physical safeguards that support confidentiality, integrity, and availability.

New roles and responsibilities are needed to manage these key program requirements for third-party cyber risk management. An understanding of how vendors impact cybersecurity is critical for this to be effective. Cyber touches every aspect of the business and is ubiquitous. Third parties are our supply chains. They are integrated with our business processes and cyber events impact the firm as the owner of the cyber risk.

Vendor's cyber risk is complex since we now have smart intercon-nected devices and systems where risk is inherited from one system to another. This was the case of Target, Facebook, and SolarWinds just to name a few. Vendors are not understood in their context and programs cannot be checklists only. They must understand how the vendor can dam-age the firm and act to prevent it. This next book is about how the business can have an effective approach to understand it and manage cyber vendor risk in context.

Notes

1 OneTrust Vendorpedia (2019, December 20). PCI DSS compliance: 3 key third-party risk management requirements. https://www.vendorpedia.com/blog/third-party-risk-requirements-for-pci-dss-compliance/.
2 PCI Security Standards Council (2016, March). Information supplement: Third-party security assurance. https://www.pcisecuritystandards.org/documents/ThirdPartySecurityAssurance_March2016_FINAL.pdf.
3 NAIC (2017). National association of insurance commissioners. https://content.naic.org/.
4 NAIC (2017, 4th quarter). Insurance data security model law. https://content.naic.org/sites/default/files/inline-files/MDL-668.pdf?39.
5 Official Journal of the European Union, Regulation (EU) 2016/679 Of the European Parliament and the Council of 27 April 2016 (2016, April 27). General data protection regulation. https://gdprinfo.eu/.
6 Xavier Becerra, Attorney General, State of California Department of Justice (2021). California Consumer Privacy Act (CCPA). https://www.oag.ca.gov/privacy/ccpa.
7 US Department of Health and Human Services (2020). Health information privacy. https://www.hhs.gov/hipaa/index.html.
8 US Department of Health and Human Services (2020). HIPAA enforcement.https://www.hhs.gov/hipaa/for-professionals/compliance-enforcement/index.html.
9 US Government Publishing Office (2013, January 25). Federal Register Department of Health and Human Services. https://www.govinfo.gov/content/pkg/FR-2013-01-25/pdf/2013-01073.pdf.
10 Pribanic and Pribanic (2019). Willful negligence legal definition. https://pribanic.com/legal-glossary/willful-negligence-legal-definition/.
11 Legal Information Institute, Cornell Law School (2020). 42 US code 1320d-6 – Wrongful disclosure of individually identifiable health information. https://www.law.cornell.edu/uscode/text/42/1320d-6.
12 US Department of Justice (2005, June 1). Scope of criminal enforcement under 42 U.S.C. 130d-6, Memorandum Opinion for the General Counsel Department of Health and Human Services and the Senior Counsel to the Deputy Attorney General. https://www.justice.gov/sites/default/files/olc/opinions/attachments/2014/11/17/hipaa_final.htm.

13 Weiser, P. (Colorado Attorney General, 2019). Consumer protection. https://coag.gov/office-sections/consumer-protection/.

14 Federal Trade Commission (2002, July 2). Gramm-Leach-Bliley Act. https://www.ftc.gov/tips-advice/business-center/privacy-and-security/gramm-leach-bliley-act.

6

HIPAA AND VENDOR CYBER RISK MANAGEMENT

HIPAA

The Health Insurance Portability and Accountability Act (HIPAA) is designed to cover risks to information security which may arise at various stages of processing of information involving the creation, receiving, maintaining, or transmitting of protected health information (PHI). The foundation of HIPAA's security rule is based on the assessment, analysis, and management of risk (including the risk posed by third parties and vendors) to ensure the protection of PHI against threats, hazards, and impermissible uses and/or disclosures.

A definition of PHI under HIPAA states that PHI comprises "any information held by a covered entity which concerns health status, the provision of healthcare, or payment for healthcare that can be linked to an individual."[1]

In simple terms, PHI includes any identifiable information by which someone could recognize an individual, including:

- Demographic data
- Contact data

DOI: 10.4324/9781003581321-8

Table 6.1 Covered Entities under HIPAA

Healthcare Providers	Any healthcare provider who electronically transmits PHI in connection with transactions defined under HIPAA Transaction Rule
Health Plans	Insurers and other entities who bear the cost of medical care
Healthcare Clearing Houses	Entities engaged in translating nonstandard information they receive from another entity into a standard format or vice versa
Business Associates	Any individual or entity that provides services to a covered entity or performs functions on its behalf that involve handling of PHI
Exceptions	A group health plan with less than 50 employees which is not otherwise a covered entity

- Medical history
- Lab and test reports
- Insurance data

Entities covered under the Act include healthcare providers, health plans, and healthcare clearing houses. It is incumbent upon these entities to also ensure that their Business Associates (BAs) (third parties such as IT, Cloud, and other service providers) must be fully compliant with the specified rules. Even though BAs are not liable under the Act, they must comply with the prescribed regulatory standards and are required to sign a Business Associate Agreement (BAA) with the covered entity to abide by applicable privacy rules and implement required safeguards. It is important to note that 'BA' under HIPAA includes all service providers who are engaged in the handling of PHI on behalf of the covered entity (Table 6.1).

Covered Entities under HIPAA

HIPAA regulations are not confined only to the protection of PHI from theft or the machinations of malicious threat actors, but to ensure protection from negligence and carelessness in the handling of PHI. Given below is a table from the HIPAA Journal – Healthcare Data Breach Statistics, 2021,

Table 6.2 Breaches by Covered Entity Type

Year	Healthcare Provider	Health Plan	Business Associate	Health Clearing House	Total
2009	14	1	3	0	18
2010	134	21	44	0	199
2011	134	19	45	1	199
2012	155	23	40	1	219
2013	191	20	64	2	277
2014	196	41	77	0	314
2015	195	61	14	0	270
2016	256	51	22	0	329
2017	285	52	21	0	358
2018	273	53	42	0	368
2019	398	59	53	2	512
2020	497	70	73	2	642
Total	2728	471	498	8	3705

Source: HIPAA Journal – Healthcare Data Breach Statistics, 2021.

that shows the breaches reported over the past 12 years.[2] From this data it is evident that BAs have suffered over 13% of the total next only to healthcare providers who account for almost 74% of the data breaches (Table 6.2).

HIPAA's basic tenets revolve around three primary rules:

1. *The Security Rule:* This rule stipulates that the covered entities and their BAs must implement the required measures to protect confidentiality, integrity, and availability of PHI through the implementation of Administrative, Physical, and Technical security measures. In effect, this involves the creation of appropriate policies and procedures, implementing control over physical access and protection of PHI in storage, use, and transit.

2. *The Privacy Rule:* This rule stipulates the guidelines under which PHI is used or disclosed as well as the privacy rights of patients, such as right to access, edit, or copy their records.

3. *The Breach Notification Rule:* This rule stipulates that in the event of a breach (leak or loss), covered entities must notify affected patients within 60 days of such an event.

In 2012, the following new provisions were added under the HIPAA Omnibus Rule:

- Rules for the use of patient data for marketing purposes.
- Exchanging PHI for payment; disclosures of PHI to individuals participating in a patient's care or payment for care.
- Disclosures related to student immunization records.
- Including certain categories of BAs and subcontractors liable for their own security breaches.
- Making it mandatory for BAs and subcontractors to comply with HIPAA privacy and security requirements.
- Requires healthcare providers to report data breaches that are deemed not harmful if they involve impermissible uses and disclosures of PHI doing away with the threshold of significant risk to a minimum of over five hundred individuals.
- Enforcement of Genetic Information Non-discrimination Act (GINA) rules which place restrictions on health plans from using genetic information for underwriting purposes and from employers using it in their hiring and promotion processes.
- Requirement that covered entities revise their BAAs to incorporate assurances regarding the compliance to the HIPAA Security Rule and that they have updated their notice of privacy practices.

From being a peripheral requirement under HIPAA, vendor risk management has now become a core activity from a risk management and compliance perspective. In the past a contractual assurance regarding security measures obtained from vendors and third parties that was considered once adequate, but the Act now places the onus on covered entities to ensure compliance through a comprehensive vendor risk management program. HIPAA requirements call for third party due diligence by covered entities but does not prescribe any particular methodology for it.

Keeping up with the regulatory requirements under HIPAA is a challenge for most healthcare providers, but now they must work more closely and directly with their BAs. This involves the understanding and monitoring of security threats and challenges and the controls and security measures deployed by each vendor for the protection of PHI. This not only enhances the scope of risk management of a covered entity to cover its vendors, but requires that processes, procedures, and technology be put in place to ensure ongoing compliance under HIPAA.

Key elements of building and implementing an effective vendor (BA) risk management program are as under:

- The program should include all BAs and their subcontractors. This is a requirement under the Omnibus Rule which states that the chain of compliance starts with the HIPAA-covered entity, through the BA, and ends with the lowest tier subcontractor.
- Conducting detailed due diligence with respect to PHI security and compliance aspects before onboarding any new vendor. All personnel who are engaged in due diligence must be fully conversant with HIPAA requirements.
- Monitoring existing vendors for compliance on an ongoing basis.
- Ascertaining the level of access to PHI so that BAs and their subcontractors can categorize and develop relevant security measures.
- Business Associates must develop their own documented set of privacy, security policies, and processes which must be done while conducting the vetting process. These should cover all employees, contractors, and other persons who are a part of their workforce.
- Contracts with BAs must cover the requirement of a HIPAA security program, conducting annual privacy/security assessments and submission of reports, termination conditions for lapses, breaches, or failure to follow HIPAA security norms.
- Implementation of physical security measures

Non-compliance with HIPAA requirements, or violations and lapses can be expensive for covered entities. Covered entities must develop a HIPAA compliant risk management program that encompasses not only their own processes and systems but those of their BAs as well.

Following the implementation of the Omnibus Rule in 2013, BAs are required to be HIPAA compliant. It also calls for a BAA to be put in place between the covered entity and the BA which clearly specifies the conditions under which information can be shared, exchanged, and transmitted. Multi-Speciality Collection Services, a BA of the Stanford University

Hospital, had accidentally compromised medical data of 20,000 patients in an email sent to a job applicant. This kind of incident shows that BA could have avoided such a security breach if they a better understanding of the HIPAA requirements and ensuring necessary controls were in put in place.[3]

Some common causes that lead to HIPAA violations are:[4]

- Unencrypted devices
- Unauthorized data access
- Negligent employees
- Theft of company devices
- Improper disposal of PHI
- Access to PHI from unsecured devices (Table 6.3)

Table 6.3 Healthcare Insurance Portability and Accounting Act at a Glance

Year of Enactment	1996 – Updated in 2013
Regulatory body	US Department of Health and Human Services
Regulated party	Covered entities are health plans, health care clearinghouses, and certain health care providers
Protected party	Patients
Protected health information	PHI – Health information that neither identifies nor provides a reasonable basis to identify an individual
Disclosure requirements	Within 60 days from date of data breach
Data security requirements	Risk Assessments, Security Standar ds Audit, Privacy Standards Audit (Not required for BAs), Asset and Device Audit, HITECH Subtitle D Privacy Audit, Physical Site Audit
Vendor program required	Yes. Covered entities and their outsourcing vendors (business associates)
Other specific requirements	A covered entity must implement technical policies and procedures that allow only authorized persons to access electronic protected health information
Civil penalties	$100–$50,000 per violation
Criminal penalties	$50,000–$250,000 fine and one to ten-year imprisonment depending on violations. The Department of Justice is responsible for criminal prosecutions

Notes

1   Blue, L. (2023, October 6). Disastrous HIPAA violation cases|7 cases to learn from. Providertech. https://www.providertech.com/disastrous-hipaa-violation-cases-7-cases-to-learn-from/.

2   Riley, S. (2023, August 8). Business associate HIPAA violation, 20,000 records breached. Compliancy Group. https://compliancy-group.com/business-associate-hipaa-violation-20000-records-breached/.

3   Team, M. (2021, February 11). Managing the HIPAA risks of outsourcing to BAs. Medsphere. https://www.medsphere.com/blog/outsourcing-managing-hipaa-risks-2/.

4   A HIPAA Compliance Checklist for Third-Party Risk Management (n.d.). Prevalent. https://www.prevalent.net/blog/hipaa-compliance-checklist/.

7

GENERAL DATA PROTECTION REGULATION (GDPR)

Implications of GDPR for the Supply Chain

As per the General Data Protection Regulation (GDPR), "third party" refers to any natural or legal person, public authority, agency, or body other than the data subject, controller, processor, and persons who, under the direct authority of the controller or processor, are authorized to process personal data.[1]

GDPR obligations on organizations and compliance are applicable regardless of their geographical location if they target, collect, and process data on European Union (EU) citizens. Business enterprises that form any part of the supply chain must adhere to GDPR provisions such as:

- Obtaining clear consent from all stakeholders across the supply chain for the collection and processing of their personal data.
- Implementing suitable security measures to ensure data security within their organization, as well as their suppliers' organizations.

DOI: 10.4324/9781003581321-9

- Including clear and explicit clauses in contracts to ensure that all third-party data processors are GDPR-compliant.
- Complying with the 72-hour breach notification requirement, which applies to both the business as well as their supply chain partners.
- Ensuring that supply chain partners are aware of the potential fines and penalties for non-compliance, which can be up to 4% of annual global turnover or €20 million, whichever is higher.

GDPR Articles and Recitals

GDPR comprises two components: the (99) articles and (173) recitals. While the articles provide legal requirements that must be adhered to, the recitals offer provides guidance on how organizations can comply with GDPR.

According to Article 24 of GDPR, the responsibility of ensuring processing compliance with GDPR Regulations rests with a data controller (an individual or organization). The controller is required to implement appropriate technical and organizational measures toward this and should be able to demonstrate that processing is performed in accordance with this Regulation. The controller must consider the nature, scope, context, and purposes of processing as well as the risks of varying likelihood and severity for the rights and freedoms of natural persons. Security measures must be reviewed and updated where necessary.

Under Recital 77, which provides guidance on the implementation of appropriate measures, and on the demonstration of compliance by the controller or the processor, especially as regards the identification of the risk related to the processing, their assessment in terms of origin, nature, likelihood and severity, and the identification of best practices to mitigate the risk (Vollmer, 2023). Third-party risks must also be conducted and considered and associated risk mitigation must be implemented.

Conducting third-party risk assessments using manual questionnaires and spreadsheets is unreliable and not scalable. Manual audits can also result in missed requirements; hence controllers must devise suitable assessment methodologies to ensure that third-party risk assessments are objective and scoring consistent.

Under GDPR when a controller uses third parties as "processors", it is the information controller (owner) who is liable for ensuring each third party has appropriate controls in place to ensure the privacy and security of personal data.

Recital 78 deals with appropriate technical and organizational measures for ensuring data protection. To demonstrate compliance, not only controllers, but also processors should adopt internal policies and implement measures which meet the principles of data protection by design and data protection by default.

Article 28 of GDPR mandates that where processing is to be carried out on behalf of a controller, the controller should only rely on processors who can provide adequate guarantees pertaining to the implementation of appropriate technical and organizational measures. These measures must meet GDPR compliance requirements and ensure the protection of the rights of the data subject (any individual person who can be identified, directly or indirectly, via an identifier).

Organizations often work with multiple third parties who may have access to personal information covered by the GDPR, such as data processors (including cloud applications), cloud hosting providers, and other service providers. Compliance with the GDPR requires a lot more than well-documented vendor agreements. It requires a complete understanding of how data is used, how it moves, and evidence of specific controls to protect personal data.

Third-party contracts must, however, stipulate that the 'processor' will assist the controller in ensuring compliance with the obligations detailed under Articles 32–36 considering the nature of processing and the information available to the processor. Articles 32–36 make the requirement of data protection and impact assessment and continuous monitoring of critical data processors obligatory for data controllers. Furthermore, it specifies that each processor relationship shall be governed by a contract or other legal act that makes the processor responsible to protect personal information. For this the required risk assessment must be conducted for each processor and adequate controls must be put in place.

Contracts with third parties must also specify that the processor makes available to the controller all information necessary to demonstrate compliance with the obligations laid down in this Article and allow for and contribute to audits, including inspections, conducted by the controller or another auditor mandated by the controller.[2] To ensure this, it is useful for processors to maintain a repository of all documentation collected and reviewed during the diligence process.

Article 32 covers the security of processing and obligates the controller and processor to implement appropriate technical and organizational measures that ensure the ongoing confidentiality, integrity, availability and resilience of processing systems and services. It further specifies that a process for testing, assessing and regularly evaluating the effectiveness of technical and organizational measures for ensuring the security of the processing must be put in place.

Recital 76 draws attention not only to the need for objective and regular risk assessments of processors, but also warns that this must not be treated as an onboarding exercise as GDPR standards warrant continuous monitoring and compliance.

Article 45 of GDPR governs transfer of personal data based on an adequacy decision. There is a restriction placed on transfer of personal data to a third country or an international organization where the Commission has decided that the third country or the international organization in question cannot or does not ensure an adequate level of protection. Controllers need to ensure that this condition is not violated even when it comes to their third parties.

The EU has been quite active when it comes to enforcing GDPR regulations and imposing fines and penalties for third-party failures. In some recent instances where organizations like British Airways, Marriott and Ticketmaster faced some of the largest GDPR fines, they put forth the argument to regulatory authorities that it was not them, but their third-party service providers, that were at fault. However, the regulatory authority did not buy their argument and stated that the engagement of third parties cannot reduce the company's degree of responsibility.[3] In another case in France, the data authority fined a data controller.

What emerges from these two instances of regulatory fines is that if the company has a contract with the third-party vendor and the data breach happened because of the vendor's failure to meet its obligations, a case could be made out where the third party could be held liable to pay damages because of its failures. However, it is also clear that the facts of each case may be different and unless there is clear evidence of the above, the data controller company will anyway be liable.

Notes

1 IAPP (n.d.). https://iapp.org/news/a/what-you-must-know-about-third-parties-under-the-gdpr-ccpa/.

2 Article 28 GDPR (n.d.). *GDPRhub*. https://gdprhub.eu/Article_28_GDPR#(c)_Measures_required_by_Article_32_GDPR.

3 Passing on fines for GDPR breaches|Bedell Cristin (n.d.). Bedell Cristin. https://www.bedellcristin.com/knowledge/briefings/passing-on-fines-for-gdpr-breaches/.

8

CALIFORNIA CONSUMER PRIVACY ACT (CCPA)

California Consumer Privacy Act and California Privacy Rights Act

In January 2023, the California Consumer Privacy Act (CCPA) was expanded and amended through the enactment of the California Privacy Rights Act (CPRA). The CPRA introduced new criteria and tighter regulations and expanded its reach to cover businesses that collected data of California residents but was not located in the state. Hence, together, the CCPA and CPRA became, in effect, national and global laws for anyone serving California users.

The first instance of the Attorney General of California levying a fine was that of the $1.2 million fine imposed on online retailer Sephora. The company violated the CCPA as they did not disclose the fact that they were selling consumer data; did not provide a 'do not sell my personal information' and opt-out button on their website, and not respecting Global Privacy Control (GPC) signals. GPC is a browser setting that sends a message to each website you visit to inform them of your privacy preferences, such as not to

DOI: 10.4324/9781003581321-10

share or sell your personal data unless you agree, to protect your privacy. A curative period of 30 days was given to Sephora, but allegedly they did not take required steps to ensure compliance during that time.[1]

Given that sharing of consumer data with service providers and third parties is a common business practice, the CCPA recognizes the importance of identifying the data flows, clarifying the roles and responsibilities of the third parties in the supply chain, and of reviewing and updating the contracts with the third parties to ensure compliance with the CCPA.

CCPA & CPRA Scope

The CCPA is applicable to any for-profit organization which collects personal data about California residents for commercial purposes or selling goods or services to California residents, provided they meet at least one of the following criteria:

- Has a gross annual revenue greater than $25 million
- Trades or receives personal information of at least fifty thousand California consumers, householders, or devices for commercial purposes or
- Generates greater than 50% of its annual revenue from the sale of personal information.

The CPRA has increased the threshold from organizations that buy, sell, or share personal information of 50,000-plus California consumers or households to 100,000 or more. Furthermore, it has set forth specific requirements on sensitive personal information (SPI) relating to the disclosure, purpose limitation, opt-out and opt-in after a previously selected opt-out. One of these requirements also includes the right to opt-out of third-party sales and sharing of personal information. The California Privacy Protection Agency (CPPA) has also been established to investigate, enforce, and amend the CPRA.

Types of information not covered under the CCPA include:[2]

- Protected Health Information (PHI) protected under CMIA or HIPAA
- Data gathered for medical research purposes
- Transfer of information to or from agencies that provide credit reports

- Personal information under the law that regulates financial institutions
- Information protected by California's law on driver's privacy, and
- Any information that is publicly accessible from government records at the federal, state, or local level.

The CPRA has expanded the definition of personal information covered under CCPA to include SPI which includes information related to race, sexual orientation, political views, etc.

Service Providers and Third Parties

Under the CCPA, there is a clear distinction between service providers and third parties. A "service provider" is defined as any legal entity that operates under a "service provider contract," operates for profit and receives/processes consumers' personal information from a business. A service provider is bound by a written contract that prohibits the legal entity from retaining, using, or disclosing the personal information for any purpose (including a commercial purpose) other than executing the tasks outlined in the contract.

A third party under CCPA is defined in the negative and by what it is not. It is not a covered business, a service provider, or a contractor.

Compliance Obligations

The CCPA aims to protect consumer data shared with service providers by imposing certain conditions and restrictions on both the business and the service provider. Some of these are:

- The business (covered organization) should inform the consumer about the categories of personal information that it discloses to its service providers for a business purpose and provide the consumer with the right to opt out of the sale of their personal information to third parties.
- The business should have a written contract in place with the service provider that specifies the purposes for which the personal information is processed, and prohibits the service provider from retaining, using, or disclosing the personal information for any other purpose.

- The service provider cannot sell, share, or disclose the personal information to any other entity, unless it is necessary to perform the services specified in the contract, or as otherwise permitted by the CCPA.
- The service provider should not use the personal information outside of its direct relationship with the business or combine it with other personal information that it has collected from other sources.
- The service provider should cooperate with the business in responding to consumer requests to access, delete, or correct their personal information, as required by the CCPA.
- The service provider is obliged to implement reasonable security measures to protect the personal information from unauthorized access, use, or disclosure.

By complying with the above rules, the CCPA seeks to ensure that service providers do not in any way misuse or compromise the privacy of the consumers.

An interesting case that came up was related to whether under CCPA a particular ad-tech organization was to be treated as a service provider or a business as the two entities have different obligations under the law. The ad tech company had in place a service provider contract with a covered entity. However, since the contract did not have specific restrictions on the use of processed personal information, the company had to update its service contract by modifying its privacy policy and offering a way for consumers to submit CCPA requests to retain its status as a service provider.[3]

To align with the rules, the company modified its privacy policy (clearly stating that it did not sell personal information), provided a way for consumers to submit CCPA requests, and updated their service provider contracts.

Accountability, Fines, and Penalties

While service providers are not directly liable under the CCPA for violating the consumer rights provisions, such as the right to access, delete, or opt out of the sale of personal information, they could face liabilities in the form of civil penalties of up to $2,500 per violation, or up to $7,500 per intentional violation, as enforced by the Attorney General for failure to comply with contractual obligations as per their contract with a business including:

- Using the shared personal information for any purpose other than the services specified in the contract.
- Selling, sharing, or disclosing the personal information to any other entity, except if it is essential to perform the services specified in the contract, or as otherwise permitted by the CCPA.
- Using the personal information outside of their direct relationship with the business or combining it with other personal information that they have collected from other sources.

The service provider could also be liable to the business for any damages caused due to breach of contract. Furthermore, the service provider could also be liable to the consumer for any harm caused by their unauthorized access, use, or disclosure of the personal information.

Covered entities under CCPA must put in place a clearly articulated vendor risk management policy which is designed to mitigate the impact of data breaches from supply chain attacks.

Covered entities must include the clauses in their contracts with service providers and third-party vendors to monitor, control, and audit how they process, manage, and protect the entrusted personal data. These clauses could include regular assessment, scans, testing, and audits.

Non-compliance of CCPA rules can result in fines and penalties that are dependent upon the severity and nature of the violation. In addition to civil penalties which can range from $2,500 per unintentional violation to $7,500 per intentional violation, consumers also have the right to initiate a private right of action which can result in statutory damages of $100–$750 per consumer per incident, or actual damages, whichever is greater, in case of a data breach. These penalties can be sizable if many records are compromised. CCPA does not prescribe a maximum limit of penalties for each violation.

While CCPA (CPRA) compliance requires compliance with several aspects of the law, violations that could result in a civil penalty include:[4]

- Not having a Privacy Policy that complies with the CCPA/CPRA.
- Not responding to consumers' inquiries about their CCPA (CPRA) rights.

- Collecting personal information without giving proper notice.
- Trading consumers' personal information without offering an opt-out.
- Treating consumers unfairly who exercise their CCPA (CPRA) rights.

More States Are Enacting Privacy Laws

While the CCPA is a flag bearer of privacy legislation in the United States, several other states have enacted similar data privacy laws. Here are the key states and highlights of their laws:

1. Virginia: The Virginia Consumer Data Protection Act (VCDPA) grants consumers rights such as access, correction, deletion, and data portability. Effective from January 1, 2023, it also mandates that businesses covered under the Act must conduct data protection assessments for activities that present a greater risk of data exposure or leakage. The Act is applicable to businesses which control or process the personal data of at least 100,000 consumers in a calendar year, or the personal data of at least 25,000 consumers, while deriving over 50% of gross revenue from the sale of that data.[5]

2. Colorado: The Colorado Privacy Act (CPA). It provides consumers with the right to access, correct, delete, and opt-out of the sale of their personal data. It also includes provisions for data protection assessments and imposes obligations on data controllers and processors. The Act came into effect on July 1, 2023.

3. Connecticut: The Connecticut Data Privacy Act also became effective on July 1, 2023. It includes consumer rights and business obligations similar to those of the CCPA.

4. Utah: The Utah Consumer Privacy Act (UCPA) came into effect on December 31, 2023. It provides consumers with the right to access, delete, and opt-out of the sale of their personal data. Like other privacy laws, it also imposes obligations on businesses to implement data security measures.

5. Iowa: The Iowa Consumer Data Protection Act will take effect on January 1, 2025. The ICDPA was created to protect the personal information of Iowa consumers and specifies civil penalties for entities that violate the new obligations and consumer rights.

6. Indiana: Indiana Consumer Data Protection Act (INCDPA) Indiana's data privacy law though signed in 2023, will become effective only on

January 1, 2026. In many ways the INCDPA is similar to data privacy laws in Virginia, Colorado, and Connecticut.[6]

7. Tennessee: Tennessee Information Protection Act (TIPA) provides significant privacy protections for consumers. However, some key provisions indicate that it is less consumer-friendly compared to the CCPA and its amendment, the CPRA. TIPA will take effect from effect July 1, 2025.

8. Oregon: The Oregon Consumer Data Privacy Act or OCDPA) law empowers consumers with rights to access, correct, delete, and opt-out of the sale of their personal data. Entities covered under the Act will need to perform data protection assessments. The OCDPA will take effect on July 1, 2024.

9. Montana: On May 19, 2023, Montana became the ninth state in the United States to enact comprehensive data privacy legislation. The Montana Consumer Data Privacy Act (MTCDPA) will become effective from October 1, 2024. When compared with other State Data Privacy Laws, MTCDPA's applicability threshold excludes entities that process the personal data of Montana consumers solely for the purpose of completing a payment transaction. It is likely that many brick-and-mortar stores that only collect payment data could be exempted.[7]

10. Texas: On June 18, Texas became the tenth US state to enact a comprehensive consumer data privacy law in the form of Texas Data Privacy and Security Act (TDPSA). Businesses regulated by the TDPSA have until July 1, 2024, to implement data protection measures to comply with the provisions of the law.[8]

All the above laws, by and large contain similar provisions for the establishment of consumer rights related to personal information and impose data protection obligations on businesses covered by them such as conducting data protection assessments and implementing appropriate controls. While each state has their own thresholds for covered entities, businesses across industries which collect, control, sell, or process personal data come under the purview of these privacy laws. However, there are also exemptions for certain data categories and entity types. The laws also define consumers' rights to access, correct, delete, and opt-out of the sale of their personal data. Further, they provide details of penalties and fines applicable for any violation of the law.

Notes

1   Cipm, M. D. (2023, March 21). An analysis of the Sephora enforcement action. Osano. https://www.osano.com/articles/sephora-enforcement-ccpa-analysis.

2   Admin (2022, December 16). CCPA vs. GDPR – Differences and similarities. Data Privacy Manager. https://dataprivacymanager.net/ccpa-vs-gdpr/.

3   Webb, A. (2023, November 8). 9 key CCPA breaches so far (And what we can learn from them). Tessian. https://www.tessian.com/blog/9-key-ccpa-breaches-so-far-and-what-we-can-learn-from-them/.

4   Bateman, R. (2024, May 12). CCPA (CPRA) penalties: What we know so far. TermsFeed. https://www.termsfeed.com/blog/ccpa-penalties/.

5   DiGiacomo, J. (2023, May 15). New data privacy Law: Virginia Consumer Data Protection Act (VCDPA). Revision Legal. https://revisionlegal.com/internet-law/new-data-privacy-law-virginia-consumer-data-protection-act-vcdpa/.

6   Cipp-Us, S. S. M. C. (2024, May 31). Iowa Consumer Data Protection Act: First Look & summary. Termly. https://termly.io/resources/articles/iowa-consumer-data-protection-act/.

7   The Montana Data Privacy Law: An Overview|Clifford Chance (n.d.). Clifford Chance. https://www.cliffordchance.com/insights/resources/blogs/talking-tech/en/articles/2023/12/the-montana-data-privacy-law-an-overview.html.

8   Cipm, M. D. (2023, December 12). The Texas Data Privacy and Security Act (TDPSA): All the basics. Osano. https://www.osano.com/articles/texas-data-privacy-and-security-act-tdpsa.

9

NEW YORK STATE DEPARTMENT OF FINANCIAL SERVICES (NYDFS) PART 500

The New York Department of Financial Services Cybersecurity Regulation

On November 1, 2023, the New York Department of Financial Services (NYDFS or the "Department") issued revised regulations (the "Second Amendment") to 23 NYCRR Part 500 (aka Part 500). These revisions constitute the most significant changes to Part 500 since it was first enacted in 2017. [1]

This regulation will take effect over the next two years with ongoing implementation of certain rules over such time. The initial updates to existing reporting requirements will go into effect by December 1, 2023, while further changes to required policies and procedures will take effect post April 2024. Proposed implementation timelines are different for each category of organizations, such as covered entities, small businesses, and Class A companies. [2]

Under the regulation, Class A Companies are "covered entities with at least $20,000,000 in gross annual revenue in each of the last two fiscal

DOI: 10.4324/9781003581321-11

years from business operations of the covered entity and its affiliates in" New York and: (1) over 2,000 employees averaged over the last two fiscal years, including employees of both the covered entity and all of its affiliates no matter where located; or (2) over $1,000,000,000 in gross annual revenue in each of the last two fiscal years from all business operations of the covered entity and all of its affiliates.[3]

The NYDFS also recognizes the importance of third parties in privacy and data protection and establishes compliance requirements and obligations for them.

Third Parties Under NYDFS

Third parties are those entities that provide services to covered entities. In the course of providing services, they have access to their non-public information or information systems of covered entities. The NYDFS is a path breaking regulation that aims to bring third parties under its ambit by imposing the following obligations on them:

- Third parties should implement a written cybersecurity policy which addresses the same issues as emphasized in the covered entity's policy, including risk assessment, access controls, data governance, and incident response.
- They should undertake periodic risk assessments and maintain audit trails of their cybersecurity performance.
- They should encrypt non-public information whether in transit or at rest, or use alternative balancing controls approved by the covered entity.
- They should inform the covered entity within 72 hours of any cybersecurity event that has a probability of materially harming the covered entity's normal operations.
- They should ensure compliance to requirements under NYDFS Act and provide annual certification to the covered entity regarding the same.

Covered entities are also obliged under the act to conduct due diligence and periodic assessments of their third parties' cybersecurity practices. In addition, they must prescribe minimum cybersecurity standards in their contracts with third parties.

The Six Key Updates to Part 500

The most significant modifications to Part 500 since it was first enacted in 2017 and established cybersecurity requirements for NYDFS can be grouped under the following six categories:

- New obligations for larger ("Class A") Companies
- Governance requirements
- Technical requirements
- Business continuity
- Breach notification obligations
- Enforcement.

New Obligations for Class A Companies

Class A companies are subject to additional cybersecurity obligations under the Final Amendment, including:

- The conduct of independent audits (both internal and external) of their cybersecurity programs at a frequency determined by their individual risk assessment.
- Class A companies are required to implement a privileged access management solution and implement an automated method of blocking commonly used passwords and monitoring privileged-access activity.
- Class A companies are required to monitor abnormal activity, including lateral movement by implementing an endpoint detection and response solution as well as a solution for centralized logging and security event alerting.

New Governance Requirements

NYDFS new amendment reinforces the strong emphasis it places on good cybersecurity governance through additional reporting and oversight requirements for CISOs, Management, and the Board.

- To strengthen the annual report to the Board by a CISO under original Part 500, the new requirements stipulate additional annual reporting on plans for remediating material inadequacies, timely reporting to the board on material cybersecurity issues, including significant cybersecurity events and noteworthy changes to the cybersecurity program.

- The Board (or senior governing body) of covered entities must exercise oversight of cybersecurity risk management in the following ways:
    - By developing sufficient understanding of cybersecurity-related matters to be able to exercise such oversight
    - Ensuring that management of a covered entity implements and maintains a cybersecurity program
    - Conducting regular reviews of management reports about cybersecurity-related matters
    - Verifying that management has allocated the required resources to maintain the cybersecurity program.

Under the new dispensation greater responsibility and accountability are placed on the CEO's and CISO's as follows:

- They must sign the annual certification of compliance.
- They must certify that the covered entity materially complied with the Part 500 requirements during the prior calendar year. This must be supported by data and documentation that demonstrates such material compliance.
- If for specific reasons the CEO and/or CISO cannot certify material compliance, then they must
    - Issue an acknowledgment that the covered entity did not materially comply with the requirements of Part 500 for the previous calendar year.
    - Specify the sections of Part 500 and describe the nature and extent of such non-compliance.
    - Define a timeline for remediation or state that confirmation that remediation has been completed.

Risk assessment is another area where new governance requirements are specified such as the conduct of annual risk assessments which must also be reviewed whenever a change in the business or technology causes a material change to the covered entity's cyber risk.

The definition of "risk assessment" under the new NYDFS amendment has been expanded to include

> the process of identifying, estimating and prioritizing cybersecurity risks to organizational operations (including mission, functions, image, and reputation), organizational assets, individuals, customers, consumers, other organizations, and critical infrastructure resulting from the operation of an information system. Risk assessments incorporate threat and vulnerability analyses and consider mitigations provided by security controls planned or in place.

NYDFS new amendment places strong emphasis on covered entities conducting incident response exercises (at least annually) based on playbooks which involve all staff and management members critical to the response process to test the effectiveness of business interruption and disaster recovery ("BCDR") plans. Such testing exercises should also cover the covered entity's ability to restore its systems from backups.

New Technical Requirements

The new amendment stipulates new technology-related obligations which are applicable to all covered entities and not just Class A companies as detailed below:[4]

- The use of MFA has been mandated as a means for any individual accessing any information of a covered entity. Any exception to this must be in the form of alternative controls which are equivalent to MFA.
- Implementation of risk-based controls designed to protect against malicious code, including those that monitor and filter web traffic and email to block malicious content.
- Removing the use of alternative compensating controls to encryption of non-public information in transit over external networks.
- In addition to performing annual penetration testing, covered entities should conduct automated scans of information systems (and a manual review of systems not covered by such scans), for the purpose of determining, analyzing, and reporting vulnerabilities at a frequency determined by the risk assessment, and promptly after any material system changes. Furthermore, they must ensure that they have a monitoring process in place for alerting and undertaking timely remediation of vulnerabilities.

- Wherever passwords are being used for authentication, they must conform to industry standards. A written policy for the use of passwords must be implemented.
- Policies and procedures for maintaining an asset inventory including a method to track key information for each asset such as asset owner, location, classification or sensitivity, support expiration date, and recovery time objectives must be clearly articulated along with the frequency required to update and validate the asset inventory.
- Covered entities must implement a policy of minimum access privileges based on only those necessary to perform the user's job function. They must further limit the number of privileged accounts, conduct at least an annual review of all user access privileges, and disable accounts that are no longer necessary.
- Protocols that permit remote control of devices must be disabled or securely configured. Also, any access must be terminated immediately following decommissioning of devices or departure of personnel.

Third-party vendors also need to align with the updated scope for security safeguards, including penetration testing, encryption, and MFA.

Incident Response and Business Continuity Planning

Even the best laid security plans and systems can be breached. Incident response and business continuity and disaster recovery (BCDR) plans are required to deal with such eventualities to mitigate disruption and damage. The new version of the NYDFS regulation recognizes the need to have incident response playbooks that will be put into action when the need to address issues like containment, eradication, and recovery from backups. Further, clear operating procedures for conducting root cause analysis as to how and why an event occurred, its business impact and determining what needs to be done to prevent reoccurrence must be defined.

Covered entities must now have a comprehensive BCDR plan to ensure the continued availability of the entity's information systems and critical services. BCDR plans must identify documents, data, facilities, IT infrastructure, services, people, and skills necessary for avoiding any disruption of operations of the covered entity's business. A prescribed communication plan that defines modes of communication with key persons in the event of a cybersecurity-related disruption must be put in place. Further, procedures for maintaining backups, timely recovery of critical data and information systems must be a part of the BCDR plan as well as assistance that may be required from third parties that are necessary to the continued operations of the covered entity's information systems.

Breach Notification Obligations

One of the key areas of most cybersecurity regulations relates to breach notification. Under the original NYDFS regulation covered entities were required to notify NYDFS within 72 hours of determining that a cyber-security event which had a reasonable likelihood of materially disrupting normal operations of the entity had occurred. Also, this also included any notification to any other regulatory body. The new regulation has further stipulated the following:

In every event of a ransomware attack on a covered ransomware must be reported. In addition, a 24-hour notification obligation is placed for any extortion payment connected to the cybersecurity incident. If an extortion payment has been made, then an explanation as to why the payment was made must be filed within a 30-day period.

A further obligation entails that covered entities must promptly pro-vide any information sought by the superintendent regarding a reported incident and that covered entities have a continuing obligation to provide updates.

It is important to note that third-party vendors involved in incidents must also adhere to these reporting timelines.

Enforcement

New enforcement provisions provide that the commission of a single act forbidden by Part 500, or the failure to satisfy an obligation, constitutes a violation. These include failure to prevent unauthorized access to non-public information due to non-compliance as well as any material failure to comply for any 24-hour period with any Part 500 obligation.

Managements along with their legal and compliance teams, must fully become conversant with a list of mitigating factors that NYDFS will consider while assessing penalties, such as cooperation, good faith, intentionality, history of prior violations, harm to customers, gravity of violation, number of violations, involvement of senior management, penalties imposed by other regulators, and the financial resources of the covered entity and its affiliates.

The NYDFS has published a set of timelines for all different classes of regulated entities since compliance requirements of the new amendment will take effect in phases.

The objective of the second amendment to The NYDFS Part 500 is focused on enhancing cybersecurity governance, reporting, and compliance, affecting both covered entities and their third-party partners. Risks related to non-compliance include financial fines (historically up to $6 million), reputational damage, and increased regulatory scrutiny.

Notes

1   Third-Party Vendor Management & NYDFS Part 500|Prevalent (n.d.). Prevalent. https://www.prevalent.net/blog/third-party-vendor-management-and-nydfs-regulation-500/.
2   NYDFS releases Major Update to Part 500 Cybersecurity Requirements for Financial Services Companies|Paul Hastings LLP (n.d.). https://www.paulhastings.com/insights/client-alerts/nydfs-releases-major-update-to-part-500-cybersecurity-requirements.
3   Marykate (2023, November 8). New York State sets the bar for cybersecurity requirements. Connect on Tech. https://www.connectontech.com/new-york-state-sets-the-bar-for-cybersecurity-requirements/.
4   Nahra, K. J., Gopinathan, A., & Jessani, A. A. (2023, November 28). NYDFS finalizes amendments to cybersecurity regulations. WilmerHale. https://www.wilmerhale.com/en/insights/blogs/wilmerhale-privacy-and-cybersecurity-law/20231128-nydfs-finalizes-amendments-to-cybersecurity-regulations.

10

DEFENSE FEDERAL ACQUISITION REGULATION SUPPLEMENT (DFARS)

Defense Federal Acquisition Regulation Supplement

Cybercriminals and adversary nation states are actively engaged in cyber espionage and a significant threat to US cyber infrastructure. In recent times, cyber-attacks have been carried out by adversaries on public and private infrastructure, which is considered critical to the safety, security, and wellbeing of citizens. This has placed the onus of safeguarding even private agencies and government agencies (which normally fall outside the purview of the Pentagon) from cyber-attacks on the DoD. In May 2021, Colonial Pipeline ransomware caused widespread concern as fuel supplies along the east coast of the United States were disrupted. The SolarWinds cyber incident that involved the use of trojanized updates by threat actors revealed gaps in US cyber defenses and showed that even branches of the military, the US State Department, and the Pentagon were vulnerable to these kind of attack vectors.

Companies working with the DoD and other federal government agencies as defense contractors are privy to confidential information.

DOI: 10.4324/9781003581321-12

The frequency of cyberattacks and their growing sophistication make it essential for any vendor organization to observe minimum security standards prescribed in the DFARS regulation to protect confidential and sensitive information that relates to their work contracts with the DoD. Compliance failures by vendors could lead to potentially serious consequences for the DoD and even national security. Therefore, the DOD is empowered to take strict actions including halting business operations for the vendors concerned if necessary.

What Is DFARS?

The main goal of DFARS is to safeguard the privacy of Controlled Unclassified Information (CUI). CUI refers to any sensitive unclassified information that requires specific safeguarding or dissemination controls. Federal agencies maintain a public registry of CUI categories and subcategories, outlining why certain information falls under the CUI designation. These designations help agencies handle and protect unclassified information effectively.[1]

DFARS and NIST Standards

The National Institute of Standards and Technology through its Special Publication 800-171 (NIST 800-171) provides a set of recommended requirements pertaining to protecting and distributing CUI data that is considered sensitive but not classified in Non-Federal Information Systems and Organizations. The Manufacturing Extension Network (MEP), a resource center for manufacturers involved in supply chains tied to government contracts also provides a NIST Self-Assessment Handbook (NIST Handbook 162) which helps organizations assess how far they are in implementing NIST SP 800-171 and becoming DFARS compliant.[2] Federal regulations including DFARS mandate that all companies dealing with CUI must evaluate and meticulously record their adherence in specific crucial domains. The following NIST SP 800-171 list shows the 14 critical security areas that are required to be addressed to pass a DFARS compliance audit:

1. Access Control
   Access control revolves around granting, restricting, and managing access to CUI. It encompasses various aspects, including physical access

to company facilities, handling CUI, system-based controls, and utilizing information processing services.

2. Awareness and Training

Raising cybersecurity awareness and providing regular training will help employees understand their security responsibilities and instill best practices in preventing errors, ensuring compliance, and identifying various cyber threats at an early stage.

3. Audit and Accountability

DoD contractors must maintain audit trails so that they can monitor, examine, investigate, and report all unauthorized, unlawful, and improper activities associated with CUI. These audit trails enable tracing specific user actions to identify the individual responsible for the unauthorized actions and hold them accountable if CUI is leaked or compromised.

4. Configuration Management

Configuration management refers to exercising controls over the configuration process to maintain the integrity of information technology systems and products. Whether it is software, hardware, or other IT assets, configuration management helps maintain performance quality and functionality by tracking and monitoring changes to configuration data.

5. Identification and Authentication

Identification and authentication are extremely critical in ensuring that only authorized users have access to CUI and other system resources. Being the first line of defense, this family of controls plays a significant role in safeguarding IT assets and infrastructure.

6. Incident Response

The absence of a well-designed incident response plan can lead to the escalation of cyber threats and attacks that could cause serious harm. An effective incident response strategy is characterized by documented playbooks which clearly articulate preparation, detection, analysis, containment, recovery, and user response activities. Apart from mitigating the impact of cyber-attacks, incident response processes also need to include communication plans that track, document, and report incidents to internal and external authorities.

7. Maintenance

System maintenance procedures involve performing preventive maintenance and corrective maintenance to ensure maximum uptime for critical systems. Failure to conduct planned system maintenance could lead to situations that could compromise the privacy and confidentiality of CUI.

8. Media Protection

Types of system media that are commonly used in an IT environment include removable hard drives, magnetic tapes, compact discs, mobile devices, and thumb drives. Policies and procedures that ensure that only authorized media is used and any access to CUI is restricted in a manner that data can neither be exfiltrated nor destroyed must be implemented.

9. Personnel Security

Personnel security aims to minimize the risk that employees pose to CUI and other company assets. By preventing exploitation or malicious use of organizational resources, contractors can safeguard sensitive data effectively. To accomplish this requires ensuring diligence when employing new workers through background checks and exercise caution during the hiring, reassignment, and termination processes. Any laxity in personnel security can pose a risk to CUI by offering an opportunity for malicious use of company resources.

10. Physical protection

Physical protection must go hand-in-hand with IT security. Protection of buildings, data centers and systems as well as their supporting infrastructure should be protected from threats related to their physical environment. Contractors working with DoD must identify and safeguard sensitive areas with closed-circuit television cameras, locks, and card readers and security personnel so that only authorized people can access these areas, thereby ensuring CUI security at all times.

11. Risk Assessment

Risk assessments are the starting point for cybersecurity initiatives. They help in identification and prioritization of risks related to protect IT assets, operations, employees, and supply chain partners of an organization. Determining vulnerabilities and security gaps on an ongoing basis is essential for protecting all key information assets including CUI from security threats and compromise attempts.

12. Security Assessment

Security assessments are similar to risk assessments. A security assessment rigorously examines your company's operational, management, and technical security requirements. These assessments serve as a critical validation mechanism, ensuring that various business components have been implemented correctly and are functioning as intended. Specifically, they verify that these components align with your infrastructure's security standards.

13. Systems and Communications Protection

    System and Communications Protection is a crucial aspect of information security. Its key components include securing organizational system boundaries through the implementation of technologies such as gateways, routers, firewalls, and network-based malicious code analysis systems, implementing encrypted tunnels within the system security architecture for enhanced protection, separation of user functionality and system management, as well as preventing unauthorized information transfer via shared resources. System and Communications Protection forms a critical layer of defense, ensuring secure information exchange within organizational systems.

14. System and Information Integrity

    Another critical aspect of safeguarding CUI is maintaining system and information security. This security area involves implementing mechanisms for error detection and correction, mitigation measures against malicious code (such as installing antivirus software), and processes to protect CUI against tampering and damage. By maintaining system integrity and promptly addressing any issues, contractors can ensure the trustworthiness and reliability of CUI.

DFARS Compliance

Achieving full compliance with DFRAS is a process that could span several months. The initial steps involve developing an understanding of the Defense Federal Acquisition Regulation Supplement (DFARS) and conducting a thorough DFARS assessment. Ultimately, achieving compliance not only fulfills the legal obligations of being a DoD contractor but also instills confidence in other business partners, assuring them that their information is securely safeguarded and well-managed.

Other requirements that are important in a DFARS compliance audit are the adoption of 79 fundamental protocols, implementing effective intrusion detection, monitoring, and cyber incident reporting and analysis.

The compliance process mandates that all contractors evaluate networks and procedures to guarantee the implementation of sufficient security measures. Compliance failures could result in the severance of contracts and severely damage work relationships with DoD and other federal agencies.

All DoD contractors as well as federal agencies are required to be DFARS-compliant. DFARS is applicable to suppliers, third parties, and contractors involved in DoD acquisitions, emphasizing the importance of cybersecurity and protection of sensitive data. It is important to note that not only prime contractors, but subcontractors and suppliers at all tiers of the supply chain must operate in line with DFRS requirements.

The minimum requirements to be considered DFRS compliant include:

- Identifying the location of sensitive information and creating a compliance team to monitor CUI while including all staff members in all processes.
- Putting in place a process for security risk assessment. Such a security assessment must be conducted two or more times per year and run whenever an organization implements a change to relevant operations.
- Implementing access controls as per the standards expressed in NIST SP800-171 and ensuring adequate security to safeguard covered defense information.
- Undertake staff training and awareness related to DFARS compliance.
- Promptly report cyber incidents and collaborate with DoD in addressing security incidents.
- Pass a readiness assessment following NIST SP 800-171 guidelines, which cover various aspects of IT information security.

DoD contractors can greatly enhance their readiness through third-party certifications such as CMMC, which is now necessary for being awarded contracts with the DoD.

Notes

1   32 CFR 2002.12 – CUI categories and subcategories (n.d.). https://www.ecfr.gov/current/title-32/subtitle-B/chapter-XX/part-2002/subpart-B/section-2002.12.
2   Spencer, T. (2019, November 15). What is the NIST SP 800-171 and who needs to follow it? NIST. https://www.nist.gov/blogs/manufacturing-innovation-blog/what-nist-sp-800-171-and-who-needs-follow-it-0.

11

FRAMEWORKS AND CERTIFICATIONS

Frameworks and Certifications

Frameworks and certifications not only enable a systemic implementation of cybersecurity initiatives, but also ensure that organizations adhere to best practices, meet regulatory requirements, and build trust with stakeholders through demonstrated commitment to security standards. Key benefits for organizations adopting frameworks and getting certified are as follows:

- Implementing best practices and standardized methods for assessing and mitigating risks, ensuring a consistent approach across different entities within the supply chain.
- Maintaining the integrity and security of the supply chain by providing guidelines on how to protect against threats such as counterfeits, unauthorized production, tampering, and theft.
- Building resilience against disruptions caused by cyber incidents, thereby ensuring continuity of operations.

DOI: 10.4324/9781003581321-13

- Certifications often signify compliance with regulatory requirements, which can be essential for organizations to operate legally or to enter certain markets.
- Enhancing trust among stakeholders, including customers, partners, and regulators, by demonstrating a commitment to cybersecurity.
- Organizations with robust supply chain risk management practices can gain a competitive edge by minimizing the risk of cyber incidents that can lead to financial loss or damage to reputation.

Examples of frameworks for management of cyber risks covered in this chapter include the following:

- The National Institute of Standards and Technology (NIST) framework which provides comprehensive guidance on managing cybersecurity risks in supply chains and helps fulfill responsibilities under US Executive Order 14028 on improving the nation's cybersecurity.
- The ISO/IEC 27001 framework is a globally recognized benchmark for information security management systems (ISMSs). This standard offers a roadmap for entities of different sizes and industries to create, apply, sustain, and progressively enhance their information security management system. Adoption and adherence to ISO/IEC 27001 signifies that an organization has established a framework for managing data security risks, in alignment with the industry's finest practices and the foundational principles of this International Standard.
- Cybersecurity Maturity Model Certification (CMMC) framework developed by the Department of Defense (DoD) is designed to enhance the protection of federal contract information (FCI) and CUI within the DIB sector. It extends the foundational DFARS 252.204-7012 mandates by integrating a third-party evaluation and certification process. This ensures that robust security protocols are consistently applied throughout the supply chain.

The choice or applicability of frameworks and certifications for supply chain cyber risk management depends on several factors such as:

- The specific security needs and requirements and business objectives of the organization.

- The legal and regulatory mandates that the organization must comply with.
- Prevailing standards and best practices within the industry.
- The types and levels of cyber risks faced by the organization and its supply chain.
- The cost of implementing and maintaining the frameworks and certifications.
- The ability of the chosen framework to integrate with the organization's existing systems and processes.
- The capacity of the framework to adapt to the growth and changes in the organization.
- The complexity of the supply chain and the need to implement the framework across all its tiers.
- The kind of relationships with suppliers and partners and their own security postures.

The above factors contribute to a comprehensive approach to managing cybersecurity risks in supply chains, ensuring the integrity, security, quality, and resilience of the supply chain and its products and services.

Overall, certifications and frameworks are essential tools for organizations to effectively manage and mitigate cyber risks in their supply chains, ensuring the security and reliability of their operations.

NIST Framework

Like all living frameworks, NIST Cybersecurity Framework (CSF) has also evolved over time to address the new and emerging cybersecurity challenges.[1] The NIST 2.0 has six core functions: Govern, Identify, Protect, Detect, Respond, and Recover as detailed in Table 11.1.

NIST 2.0

The NIST CSF offers comprehensive guidelines as well as best practices that can be adopted by organizations to improve information security and cybersecurity risk management. NIST CSF is a voluntary standard which is flexible enough to integrate with the existing security processes within any organization, in any industry.

Table 11.1 NIST 2.0 Core Functions

GOVERN	The policies, procedures, and processes to manage and monitor the organization's regulatory, legal, risk, environmental, and operational requirements are understood and inform the management of cybersecurity risk.
IDENTIFY	The key information assets and processes that need to be protected
PROTECT	Implement appropriate controls and protection mechanisms
DETECT	Put in place mechanisms to identify cyber threats and attacks
RESPOND	Develop suitable response mechanisms to mitigate the impact of cyber incidents
RECOVER	Implement processes to restore services impaired by adverse impacts of cyber incidents

The NSF 2.0 in a departure from its US-centric approach, aims to cast a wider net, and aims to serve organizations across the globe. The new version of the framework was released on February 26, 2024 and has a broader scope that incorporates references to the NIST Privacy Framework, the NICE Workforce Framework for Cybersecurity, and the Secure Software Development Framework. This enables organizations to seamlessly integrate CSF 2.0 with their existing frameworks. The expanded list of core functions and corresponding categories of the NIST 2.0 are shown in Table 11.2.[2]

NIST CSF 2.0 has several improvements over the earlier NIST CSF 1.1 version. The first change is the expanded scope which now focuses on all organizations and does not limit itself to those operating in critical sectors. The addition of a Govern function in CSF 2.0 acknowledges the role of governance within the cybersecurity domain. The Govern function encompasses organizational context, risk management strategy, supply chain risk management, clear definition of roles and responsibilities, as well as policies and procedures. The introduction of this function will enable organizations to develop a strong cybersecurity posture.

The renewed importance of supply chain risk management in the framework is aimed at securing increasingly complex and interconnected supply chains which in recent times have seen an increasing number of supply

Table 11.2 List of Core Functions and Corresponding Categories

NIST 2.0	CYBERSECURITY FRAMEWORK	
CSF Core Function	Category	
Govern (GV)	Organizational Context	GV. OC
	Risk Management Strategy	GV. RM
	Roles and Responsibilities	GV. RR
	Policies	GV. PO
	Oversight	GV. OV
	Cybersecurity Supply Chain Risk Management	GV. SC
Identify	Asset Management	ID. AM
	Risk Management	ID. RM
	Improvement	ID. IM
Protect	Identity Management, Authentication, and Access Control	PR. AA
	Awareness and Training	PR. AT
	Data Security	PR. DS
	Platform Security	PR. PS
	Technology Infrastructure Resilience	PR. IR
Detect	Continuous Monitoring	DE. CE
	Adverse Event Analysis	DE. AE
Respond	Incident Management	RE. MA
	Incident Analysis	RE. AN
	Incident Response, Reporting, and Communication	RE. CO
	Incident Mitigation	RE. MI
Recover	Incident Recovery, Plan Execution	RC. RP
	Incident Recovery, Communication	RC. CO

Source: https://nvlpubs.nist.gov/nistpubs/CSWP/NIST.CSWP.29.pdf.

Table 11.3 CSF 2.0 Supply Chain Risk Management Cybersecurity Requirements

Cybersecurity Supply Chain Risk Management (GV.SC):
Organizational stakeholders must identify, establish, manage, monitor, and continuously improve cyber supply chain risk management processes
GV.SC-01: Organizational stakeholders should establish and mutually agree upon a Cybersecurity Supply Chain Risk Management program, strategy, objectives, policies, and processes
GV.SC-02: Roles and responsibilities related to cybersecurity for suppliers, customers, and partners should be defined, communicated, and coordinated both within the organization and externally
GV.SC-03: Integration of Cybersecurity Supply Chain Risk Management into the broader context of cybersecurity, enterprise risk management, risk assessment, and continuous improvement processes must be undertaken
GV.SC-04: Suppliers must be identified, classified, and prioritized based on their criticality.

Source: https://csf.tools/reference/nist-cybersecurity-framework/v2-0/gv/gv-sc/.

chain cyber-attacks. CSF 2.0 emphasizes the importance of evaluating their suppliers' cybersecurity practices and developing comprehensive risk management strategies that extend beyond their own enterprise security operations. Table 11.3 shows specific action points under the Cybersecurity Supply Chain Risk Management category.[3]

An important aspect of CSF 2.0 is the detailed guidance on how to develop metrics and benchmarks that accurately reflect the effectiveness of their cybersecurity practices. These metrics call for a data and analytics-driven strategy approach to security decision-making.

Among other aspects of CSF 2.0 is the enhanced emphasis on integrating cybersecurity risk management into organization-wide risk management strategies, practical guidance on achieving the framework's subcategories, and the need for continuous improvement.

CSF 2.0 requires that all the functions should be addressed concurrently, and actions that support Govern, Identify, Protect, and Detect should happen continuously while Respond and Recover actions should come into play when cybersecurity incidents occur.

Depending on the maturity and compliance with the framework an organization can choose to use the Tiers to inform its Current and Target Profiles.

Table 11.4 The Tiers – CSF Cybersecurity Risk Governance and Management

Tier	Maturity Level	Characteristics
Tier 1	Partial	Informal, Ad hoc responses
Tier 2	Risk Informed	Corporate executives are aware of risks but responses and ad hoc
Tier 3	Repeatable	Equipped to deal with vulnerabilities, cybersecurity risks, and threats
Tier 4	Adaptive	Adaptive policies and procedures, and machine learning-powered detection and response capabilities. Continuously improving

Source: The NIST Cybersecurity Framework (CSF) 2.0 (2024). https://doi.org/10.6028/nist.cswp.29.

Each Tier provides an understanding of the rigor of their cybersecurity risk governance and management practices. They also provide context for an organization's approach to cybersecurity risks and the processes in place to manage those risks (Table 11.4).

It is important to note that CSF 2.0 not only enhances focus on supply chain risk management but also on privacy risks, secure software development practices, integrating threat intelligence with security information and event management (SIEM) systems, and software supply chain management.

Given that organizations use a multitude of software products and applications there is a need to prevent and mitigate software vulnerabilities to reduce overall supply chain risk. Most software projects today rely on third-party libraries and components. Threat actors have become adept at exploiting vulnerabilities in these dependencies to compromise the overall software supply chain.

To address this, NIST provides eight best practices for comprehensive Software Supply Chain Risk Management which organizations can adopt (Table 11.5).[4]

NIST guidelines incorporate extensive vendor and supplier risk management capabilities. Apart from the above best practices, NIST recommends rigorous risk assessments, audits, and the inclusion of security requirements in contractual agreements to safeguard against potential data breaches originating from external partners.

Table 11.5 Best Practices for Supply Chain Risk Management – NIST

Identify and Manage Software Components	Prepare a SBOM used in your products and services.
Assess Software Suppliers	Gauge the security practices of your software suppliers.
Secure Software Development and Delivery Processes	Implement secure development practices.
Monitor Software Components	Continuously monitor software components for vulnerabilities.
Assess and Monitor Software Products	Evaluate the security of software products before and after deployment.
Respond to Vulnerabilities	Implement a place to address vulnerabilities promptly.
Secure Software Distribution and Installation	Ensure secure distribution and installation of software.
Secure Software Maintenance and Retirement	Manage software throughout its life cycle.

Source: https://www.scrut.io/post/nist-recommendations-software-supply-chain-attacks.

In summary, NIST CSF 2.0 offers several benefits for organizations looking to enhance their cybersecurity posture including an up-to-date approach to manage cyber risks. It also helps organizations identify, assess, and prioritize risks effectively. Furthermore, it enables organizations to align with leading industry standards and best practices.

SBOM Management

Software Bill of Materials (SBOM) management has moved to center stage post the Solar Winds and Kaseya cyber-attacks. An SBOM is essentially a nested inventory that lists the constituents making up software components. It provides detailed information about the various components used within an organization's products.

The US White House Executive Order 14028 is a directive meant for all software vendors to the US government to list the components that they used to create their products with software bill of materials documentation latest by September 2023.

It also calls for maintaining accurate and up-to-date data provenance (i.e., origin) of software code or components and controls on internal and third-party software components, tools, and services present in software development processes, and performing audits and enforcement of these controls on a recurring basis.[5]

Proactive management of SBOMs helps in knowing the components of a software product or application and managing security risks related to third-party components and dependencies. Several new regulations and standards (such as NIST, NIS Directive, and others) emphasize SBOM adoption for better cybersecurity practices.

The SBOM management process involves four steps: Generation, Storage, Analysis, and Monitoring. As new versions or builds of software are released, related SBOMs also need to be updated. This is best achieved by automating the SBOM process.

The NIS Directive for Europe

The NIS Directive for Europe is a specific directive related to cybersecurity known as the Network and Information Security (NIS) Directive. It aims to develop a common level of cybersecurity across EU Member States through collaboration, harmonization, and better crisis management.

The NIS Directive (Directive (EU) 2022/2555), came into force on January 16, 2023, replacing the previous Directive (EU) 2016/1148. The new directive encourages Member States to address new security areas, such as supply chain security, vulnerability management, core internet infrastructure, and cyber hygiene. It also establishes a cyber crisis management structure called 'CyCLONe.'

European Union Agency for Cybersecurity (ENISA) plays a key role in aiding Member States in implementing the NIS Directive through working groups and organizing cybersecurity exercises.

The EU has the NIS Directive, which is similar to what the United States has developed in terms of the NIST Framework for Improving Critical Infrastructure Cybersecurity.

The ISO/IEC 27001 is unarguably the most widely adopted standard global standard for ISMSs. The latest version of this standard is the ISO/IEC 27001:2022 and was released in October 2022. Organizations big and small across industry sectors and geographies use ISO/IEC 27001 to manage risks related to the security of data they own or handle. This standard enables organizations to proactively identify and address vulnerabilities as well as security gaps and promote cyber-resilience by implementing best practices.

ISO 27001:2022

ISO 27001 is also applicable to any organization that handles sensitive information, regardless of its size, profitability level, or industry. Following its methodology, an organization can prevent adverse cyber incidents by ensuring responsible employee security behavior and implementing robust information security practices.

Key aspects of the ISO 27001 are:

1. ISO 27001 enables organizations to adopt a risk-based approach to information security.
2. ISO 27001 follows the Plan-Do-Check-Act (PDCA) cycle for continuous improvement. In the 'Plan' step, organizations define objectives and assess risks. The 'Do' step involves implementing controls and processes. The 'Check' Stage is for monitoring and measuring performance and in the 'Act' stage corrective actions are taken to improve the system.
3. ISO/IEC 27001:2022 outlines a comprehensive set of security controls which are categorized into four domains. These are:
   - People (eight controls): these controls pertain to personnel, roles, and responsibilities within the realm of information security. Some examples include access management, training, and awareness programs. These measures are crucial for maintaining a secure and well-protected environment.
   - Organizational (37 controls): these controls place emphasis on organizational processes, policies, and governance. They include areas like risk management, asset management, and incident response.
   - Technological (34 controls): these include technological controls such as encryption, network security, and vulnerability management.
   - Physical (four controls): these controls relate to physical security measures for facilities, equipment, and data centers. These controls

cover areas such as access control, environmental protection, and secure disposal.

4. In addition to the above, ISO 27001 extends to information security controls, emphasizes the role of Senior Management, asset classification and management, documentation of security policies and procedures, and employee awareness and training.

5. In ISO/IEC 27001:2022, there are specific provisions related to supply chain management and information security in supplier relationships. ISO 27001 mandates the establishment of an information security policy for supplier relationships. This policy should cover an organization's requirements for mitigating risks associated with any supplier's access to its IT assets. Supplier Relationships are covered under Annex A.15 which includes controls related to supplier selection, contractual agreements, and monitoring.

Certification and Audit

Both NIST and ISO 27001:2022 provide a comprehensive framework for managing information security across organizations, addressing risks (including supply chain risks), and protecting sensitive data and enabling continuous improvement. Where ISO 27001 is fundamentally different from NIST is that certification requires a third-party audit of its ISO implementation. To obtain certification, organizations must demonstrate commitment to security and compliance with legal, regulatory, and contractual requirements. The third-party audit is conducted by trained ISO assessors and provides all stakeholders with the confidence that the organization has requisite systems and controls as prescribed under ISO guidelines for information security and data protection.

Cybersecurity Maturity Model Certification Framework

The CMMC framework and model was developed by the Office of the US Under Secretary of Defense for Acquisition and Sustainment of the United States Department of Defense through Carnegie Mellon University, The Johns Hopkins University Applied, Physics Laboratory LLC, and Futures, Inc. The aim of the CMMC framework is to strengthen the security posture of organizations involved in defense contracts.[6]

The CMMC framework is built upon the DFARS 252.204-7012 requirements. One major distinction is that while DFARS relies on self-assessment, CMMC requires third-party audit and certification component.

Compliance with the CMMC framework requires organizations to identify, assess, prioritize, and respond to risks. In November 2021, CMMC 2.0 was released which includes several updates to the CMMC 1.0 model that address the following aspects:

• Ensuring that sensitive information such as US FCI and CUI is protected.
• Increasing accountability while minimizing barriers to conform with DoD requirements.
• Improving DIB cybersecurity since it is the target of more frequent and complex cyber-attacks.
• Enhancing collaborative culture of cybersecurity and cyber-resilience.

There are two types of sensitive information that CMMC is focused on protecting – CUI and FCI.

CUI as per CMMC is the information that the government determines requires protection or dissemination controls. CUI is further categorized as Basic CUI (that requires basic protection measures to protect the information from unauthorized disclosure) such as information about government contracts, sensitive but unclassified information, or information that requires protection under federal laws, regulations, or executive orders as Specified CUI (that requires additional protection measures to protect the information from unauthorized disclosure) such as information related to national security and law enforcement, or any other information that requires special protection under specific laws or regulations (Table 11.6).

FCI under CMMC is any information that is not intended for public release. This comprises information that is provided by or generated for the government under a contract to develop or deliver a product or service

Table 11.6 Examples of Controlled Unclassified Information

Personally Identifiable Information (PII)	Protected Health Information (PHI)	Export-controlled or International Trade Data
Intellectual Property	Contractor-sensitive Information	Proprietary Business Information (PBI)

Table 11.7 CMMC Levels

Level 1	Foundational	To qualify for this level of protection, organizations must implement basic cybersecurity measures, such as identity management, access control, and data protection.
Level 2	Advanced	At this level of protection, organizations should have implemented more advanced security measures, such as system authentication and encryption.
Level 3	Expert	This level is indicative of high-level protection including most advanced security measures, such as continuous monitoring and security incident response plans.

Source: Kiteworks (2024, April 1). CUI CMMC: Key points & implications. Kiteworks|Your Private Content Network. https://www.kiteworks.com/risk-compliance-glossary/cmmc-cui-and-what-it-means/.

to the government, but not provided by the government to the public (such as that which exists on public websites).[7]

The objective of incorporating CMMC 2.0 standards into acquisition programs of the Department of Defense ensures that contractors and subcontractors will meet its cybersecurity requirements.

The CMMC 2.0 framework consists of 14 cyber security domains, three less than its previous version – CMMC 1.0. A domain can be described as a distinct group of security practices which are similar to each other when it comes to protecting FCI and CUI, either individually or in combination.

Other major update in CMMC 2.0 over CMMC 1.0 is that the number of levels has been reduced to three from the earlier five levels. CMMC maturity assessments have been done away with completely. Furthermore, CMMC 2.0 is dependent upon NIST SP 800-171 (as required by DFARS 252.204-7012) to qualify for CMMC levels 1 and 2. Controls from NIST SP 800-172 must be added to achieve CMMC level 3. The NIST SP 800-171 is based on security domains, practices, and processes which can be combined with organizational capabilities to develop best practices for the protection of CUI and FCI.

The key objective and purpose of CMMC is to strengthen the security posture and culture among defense contractors. It uses a combination of various standards and requirements to assess the cybersecurity maturity of the defense supply chain. DoD contractors are required to undergo formal third-party audits of their security practices by independent third-party assessors accredited by CyberAB (the CMMC accreditation body). Under this dispensation, primary contractors are accountable for ensuring security across their entire supply chain. They are required to validate subcontractor compliance with appropriate security requirements before contract award.

In summary, CMMC focuses on protection of CUI and FCI, standardizes cybersecurity practices, promotes supply chain security, and ensures compliance with growing and evolving threats in defense contracts.

Notes

1   The NIST Cybersecurity Framework 2.0 (2023). https://doi.org/10.6028/nist.cswp.29.ipd.

2   The NIST Cybersecurity Framework (CSF) 2.0 (2024). https://doi.org/10.6028/nist.cswp.29.

3   National Institute of Standards and Technology (2024). The NIST Cybersecurity Framework (CSF) 2.0. In NIST CSWP 29 [Report]. https://nvlpubs.nist.gov/nistpubs/CSWP/NIST.CSWP.29.pdf.

4   Manpreet & Manpreet (2024, January 18). Alam (2024, January 18). NIST Guidelines: Safeguarding from software supply chain attacks - Scrut Automation. Scrut Automation. https://www.scrut.io/post/nist-recommendations-software-supply-chain-attacks.

5   House, W. (2021, May 12). Executive Order on Improving the Nation's Cybersecurity. The White House. https://www.whitehouse.gov/briefing-room/presidential-actions/2021/05/12/executive-order-on-improving-the-nations-cybersecurity/.

6   CMMC (n.d.). Smithers. https://www.smithers.com/services/audit/cybersecurity-maturity-model-certification.

7   US DOD launches comprehensive CMMC 2.0 Cybersecurity Framework (n.d.). ISACA. https://www.isaca.org/resources/news-and-trends/industry-news/2022/us-dod-launches-comprehensive-cmmc-2-cybersecurity-framework.

12

ATTESTATIONS AND ASSESSMENT UTILITIES

The Snowball Effect

Many industries face ongoing challenges as both customers and vendors grapple with the cascading impact of heightened regulatory demands for transparency. Vendors are stumbling with exponentially growing questionnaire and audit requests, while customers struggle to keep compliance with their stated risk assessment targets. In fact, many medium and large enterprises have dedicated teams on both sides of chasing vendors and answering requests as a vendor.

To help the industry, there have been numerous efforts to standardize and reuse vendor due diligence information. So far, many approaches are gaining traction, but none have reached sufficient critical mass to make a dent in growing customer-to-vendor due diligence requests (Table 12.1).

DOI: 10.4324/9781003581321-14

Table 12.1 Certification Approaches Table

Approach	Description	Notable Examples
Attestation reports/ certifications	Audit reports performed by independent audit firms to provide assurance	SOC 2, ISO 27001
Questionnaire standards	A collection of questions, controls, and/or control objectives	Standardized Information Gathering Questionnaire (SIG™) by Shared Assessments, National Institute of Standards and Technology – NIST SP 800-171
Domain-specific standards	Frameworks or questionnaires developed for specific industries, use cases, or geographies	The Clearing House standard for Financial data aggregators,[a] UK Finance and IHS Markit Supplier Assurance Framework,[b] AITEC™ AIMA™,[c] NATF Supply Chain Security Assessment Model[d]
Shared Assessment Utilities	Commercial businesses that focus on conducting and reusing vendor risk assessments for multiple customers	S&P Global KY3P®, VenMinder™, ProcessUnity™, OneTrust™

a "Financial Industry Leaders Launch New Streamlined Data Sharing Risk Assessment Service", The Clearing House, January 26, 2021, https://www.theclearinghouse.org/payment-systems/articles/2021/01/01-26-2021_new-streamlined-data-sharing-risk-assessment-service.
b "New Financial Services Supplier Assurance Framework launched by UK Finance and KY3P® by IHS Markit", IHS Markit, February 24, 2022, https://ihsmarkit.com/research-analysis/new-financial-services-supplier-assurance-framework-launched.html.
c "About AITEC", AITEC.org, https://www.aitec.org/about.
d "Supply Chain Security Assessment Model Version 2.0 Document ID: 1302", North America Transmission Forum (NATF), June 4, 2021, https://www.natf.net/docs/natf/documents/resources/supply-chain/supply-chain-security-assessment-model.pdf.

Attestation Reports and Certifications

The terms such as assurance reports, independent control attestations, certifications are used somewhat interchangeably based on context. SOC 1 attestations are performed by audit firms to independently assess presence and integrity of internal controls. The assurance for the SOC reports is conducted against a set of standards established by the American Institute of Certified Public Accountants (AICPA). The SOC 1 report covers internal control environments relevant to a service organization's client's financial statements. For purposes of cyber security vendor risk assessments, it's only marginally relevant since it doesn't have specificity typically expected. The SOC 2 report covers a service organization's controls that are relevant to its operations and compliance. It's often requested and leveraged as part of a vendor risk assessment. The main difference between SOC 2 and SOC 3 is that a SOC 3 is intended for a general audience. SOC 3 reports essentially cover the same content as SOC 2 reports but are shorter and do not include the same details as a SOC 2 report. Due to their more general nature, SOC 3 reports can be shared openly and posted on a company's website. Summary of SOC 1, SOC 2, and SOC 3 reports are highlighted on the AICPA website.[1] There are other less frequently encountered types of SOC reports such SOC for supply chain and SOC for cybersecurity. SOC for supply chain focuses on controls within the entity's system relevant to security, availability, processing integrity, confidentiality, or privacy to enable users to better understand and manage the risks arising from business relationships with their supplier and distribution networks. SOC for cybersecurity focuses on the entity's cybersecurity risk management program. A good comparison of these SOC reports is covered by AICPA Comparison of SOC Examinations and Related Reports.[2]

Similarly, ISO 27001 is arguably the most popular certification, providing requirements for more than a dozen standards, especially information security management system (ISMS).[3] Using these standards enables organizations to manage appropriate security of the control environment, protecting integrity of assets such as financial information, intellectual property, employee details, or information entrusted by third parties.

Confusion and misconceptions often arise regarding the reliance on SOC 2 reports and ISO 27001 certifications for vendor assessments. In short, SOC 2 reports vary significantly in quality and coverage. Just having an SOC 2 report shouldn't give anyone a false perception of security. We cover SOC 2 reports in detail in Chapter 13. ISO 27001 certification is an even worse match to rely on for a vendor assessment due to its lack of specificity toward products & services. In Chapter 11 we do a deep dive on ISO 27001 certifications.

Questionnaire Standards

By far the most popular questionnaire standard is a SIG (Standardized Information Gathering Questionnaire by Shared Assessments).[4] SIG essentially consists of a set of standardized questions across 18 control domains that vendors share with customers. SIG questions are carefully mapped to common industry frameworks and regulations. There are two versions of the SIG:

• *SIG Core*: full library of questions that security teams can pick and choose from.
• *SIG Lite*: a condensed version of the questionnaire typically targeting lower risk vendors. Sig Lite takes the high-level concepts and questions from the larger SIG questionnaire, distilling them down to fewer questions.

SIG requires annual membership fees and comes with robust tooling, training, and instruction manuals. It's a good source of information if you are looking for self-attested responses. It's worth the effort to map SIG questions to your process to avoid unnecessary back and forth. SIG is typically updated annually, and the mapping should include the latest and prior year's version.

National Institute of Standards and Technology – NIST SP 800-171[5] is a popular source of cybersecurity vendor questionnaires with 14 security objectives, covering numerous controls each. NIST Publication 800-171, Protecting Controlled Unclassified Information in Nonfederal Systems and Organizations (NIST SP 800-171), provides federal agencies with a set of guidelines designed to ensure that Controlled Unclassified Information (CUI) remains confidential, available, and unchanged in nonfederal systems and organizations. Additionally, NIST SP 800-171 plays a pivotal role in achieving FISMA and FedRAMP compliance. While NIST SP 800-171 was designed for companies that work under a government contract, it has been commonly updated as a go to framework for cybersecurity in general.

There is no such thing as the best questionnaire standard. In Chapter 15 we discuss best practices in designing your questionnaire that's fit for purpose for your vendor risk management program.

Domain-Specific Standards

An often-overlooked opportunity lies in industry or domain-specific standardization. For example, in January 2021, The Clearing House (a banking association and payments company) facilitated a new risk assessment standard specific to financial applications and financial data aggregators.[6] The standard was backed by some of the largest financial data aggregators, numerous banks, and two prominent financial industry assessment utilities.

In the Alternative Investments Industry, AITEC™ partnered with the Alternative Investment Management Association (AIMA™) in 2016 to develop and promote AITEC-AIMA DDQ (Due Diligence Questionnaire).[7] As of March 2022, over 150 global vendors offer DDQ to AITEC and AIMA members.[8]

In the United Kingdom, UK Finance and IHS Markit (now S&P Global) partnered to develop a supplier assurance framework[9] with focus on operational resilience. It's a good example of a practical implementation how the framework provides a sound foundation for a "pooled audit" encouraged in Prudential Regulation Authority (PRA) Supervisory Statement SS2/21 as being efficient and less disruptive for the industry.[10]

In the energy sector, North America Transmission Forum (NATF) established the Supply Chain Security Assessment model.[11] It's a collaborative industry effort to streamline compliance with regulations such as CIP-013-1 – Cyber Security – Supply Chain Risk Management.[12]

The critical challenge with domain-specific standards is adoption. While it's always well-intentioned, often the standard competes with other mainstream industry standards, or in practice is difficult to implement. Industry participants who are typically passionate to contribute their time and intellectual capital in developing the standard, may not account for resource requirements to actually push standard adoption across the industry.

Engaging with Industry-Shared Assessment Utilities

An emerging approach is to work with industry-shared assessment utilities such as S&P Global KY3P®, VenMinder™, and ProcessUnity™. Each of the utilities has their specific framework and has an established commercial model. While there are multiple variations, the basic concept works something like this:

- Utility conducts a vendor assessment or completes a questionnaire on behalf of one or more customers.
- Other customers can request access to a completed vendor risk assessment or questionnaire.

The top 3 marketed benefits for customers include:

- Time to market, especially if an assessment/questionnaire is already available.
- Cost (since the cost is mutualized among multiple customers, it's expected to be more efficient than each customer absorbing expense of conducting an assessment themselves).
- Consistency (since framework is used by multiple customers there is strength in numbers when it comes to best practices, and since the cost is mutualized utility can typically invest in more controls to ensure quality).

The top 3 marketed benefits for vendors include:

- Accelerated revenue (get faster through procurement process with a pre-existing assessment report available that often acts as a seal of approval)
- Cost (one assessment is reused multiple times, avoiding unnecessary unilateral assessment requests)
- Customer satisfaction (perception of easier to do business with and security transparency)

Key shared assessment utility selection considerations:

- *Adoption*: how many other customers and vendors are part of the utility, and how many assessments by type are available "off the shelf". Some utilities will be willing to conduct assessments for vendors of your choice even if you are a sole customer, but other utilities will be selective in what new vendors they work with. If a utility is willing to share their specific lists, then you can make a more tailored determination of how close the inventory aligns. It's important to recognize that customers are key to driving the utility's adoption of new vendors, and you are expected to leverage your commercial relationships to get your vendors to work with the utility – that's how there is a win-win longer term.

- *Framework*: how robust the framework is and how well does it map to industry standards and regulations. If you are not willing to change your framework then you will need to determine how closely it aligns to your current requirements. Typically, the value of working with a utility is to adopt their framework and best practices or at a minimum map it to your overall framework. Alternatively, if utility can provide readily available data that only satisfies your partial framework requirements, it may still be advantageous to engage and streamline your overall effort.

- *Turnaround Time*: what is the expected turnaround for vendors by each assessment and questionnaire type. Although it may sound counterintuitive, it may actually be slower in some cases for a utility to onboard a new vendor than you perform the work yourself. Utilities have their terms and conditions that they need vendors to agree to and convince vendors of their value proposition, as unfortunately some vendors remain unsold on a prospect of doing yet another assessment without a guaranteed reuse.

- *Tailoring for Products and Services*: how is an assessment conducted on a company-wide level or each individual service. Company-wide assessments are typically much less useful since you will still need to conduct an assessment for services you actually consume.

- *Additional Services*: what additional value-added solutions and services are offered. Best in class providers offer a full range of third-party risk solutions that make adoption streamlined. For example, third-party risk platform, remediation services, custom assessments, managed services, cybersecurity rating monitoring.

As you can see, the value proposition is there for shared assessment utilities, but it may be wasteful to engage with one or more utilities without strong vendor adoption and a framework that can be mapped to your standards. After many years, utilities now have gained sufficient traction to be taken seriously but not yet seriously enough to replace the bulk of bespoke vendor assessment volume. We expect that trajectory to continue.

Determining Which Standards to Adopt

For robust vendor risk programs, it's advantageous to leverage popular attestation reports (at a minimum SOC 2 and ISO 27001), the SIG, relevant domain-specific standards, and work with one or more relevant shared assessment utilities. Failing to engage otherwise and insisting on getting responses to all of your questionnaires and bilateral assessment requests is wasteful for all parties involved. To work with each standard, it is important to map specifics to your framework and develop operating procedures on how to consume each standard within your assessment process. Since each standard takes some effort to integrate into your program and maintain, we don't recommend that you blindly integrate less frequently used standards without cost benefit analysis.

The answer is similar on the other side, of leveraging standards & certifications to respond to customer due diligence and vendor audit requests. You should consider prioritizing where your customers find the most value. Our recommendation is to consider getting popular attestation reports (such as a SOC 2 and/or ISO 27001), the SIG, relevant domain-specific standards, and work with one or more relevant shared assessment utilities. In Chapters 19 and 20 we cover vendor audits and best practices on how to streamline that overall process.

Notes

1 "SOC for Service Organizations: Information for Service Organizations", AICPA. org, https://us.aicpa.org/interestareas/frc/assuranceadvisoryservices/service-organization-smanagement.

2 "Comparison of SOC for Supply Chain, SOC 2, and SOC for Cybersecurity Examinations and Related, AICPA.org, Reports", AICPA.org, May 11, 2020, https:// us.aicpa.org/content/dam/aicpa/interestareas/frc/assuranceadvisoryservices/ downloadabledocuments/comparison-of-soc-examinations-and-related-reports. pdf.

3 "ISO/IEC 27001 INFORMATION SECURITY MANAGEMENT", ISO.org, November 2022, https://www.iso.org/isoiec-27001-information-security.html.

4 "Standardized Information Gathering Questionnaire", Shared Assessments, https://sharedassessments.org/sig/.

5 "Protecting Controlled Unclassified Information in Nonfederal Systems and Organizations", NIST.gov, February 2020, https://csrc.nist.gov/publications/ detail/sp/800-171/rev-2/final.

6 "Financial Industry Leaders Launch New Streamlined Data Sharing Risk Assessment Service", The Clearing House, January 26, 2021, https://www.theclearinghouse.org/

payment-systems/articles/2021/01/01–26–2021_new-streamlined-data-sharing-risk-assessment-service.

7 "The AITEC-AIMA Due Diligence Questionnaire (DDQ)", AITEC.org, https://www.aitec.org/ddq/.

8 "About AITEC", AITEC.org, https://www.aitec.org/about.

9 "New Financial Services Supplier Assurance Framework launched by UK Finance and KY3P® by IHS Markit", IHS Markit, February 24, 2022, https://ihsmarkit.com/research-analysis/new-financial-services-supplier-assurance-framework-launched.html.

10 "SS2/21 Outsourcing and third party risk management Supervisory Statement 2/21", Bank of England, March 29, 2021, https://www.bankofengland.co.uk/prudential-regulation/publication/2021/march/outsourcing-and-third-party-risk-management-ss.

11 "Supply Chain Security Assessment Model Version 2.0 Document ID: 1302", North America Transmission Forum (NATF), June 4, 2021, https://www.natf.net/docs/natf/documents/resources/supply-chain/supply-chain-security-assessment-model.pdf.

12 "CIP-013-1 – Cyber Security – Supply Chain Risk Management", NERC, October 18, 2018, https://www.nerc.com/pa/Stand/Reliability%20Standards/CIP-013-1.pdf.

13

SOC 2 REPORT

Overview of SOC 2 Report

In a prior chapter, we introduced the concept of vendor certifications and explained how a SOC 2 report is a popular choice for assuring customers about the security of your control environment. It is a go-to request and often an expectation when assessing a vendor. There is an entire industry of producing and maintaining these SOC 2 reports, and a line of audit firms happy to help. SOC 2 report has a long history preceding modern vendor risk regulations, and stems from legacy audit products such as SAS 70, SSAE 16, and SSAE 18.[1]

It is also a common trap of giving inexperienced customers a false sense of security by just relying on an SOC 2 report as part of a vendor due diligence process. In this chapter we will explain in detail the ins and outs of the SOC 2 report and how to think of it as a customer and a vendor.

The SOC 2 report covers a service organization's controls that are relevant to its operations and compliance. SOC 2 (and all SOC) attestations are performed by audit firms to independently assess the presence and integrity

DOI: 10.4324/9781003581321-15

of internal controls. The assurance for the SOC reports is conducted against a set of standards established by the American Institute of Certified Public Accountants (AICPA).

SOC 2 report can cover five Trust Service Criteria (TSC). The Security TSC is always required and referred to as "Common Criteria."

1. *Security*: ensures information security against unauthorized access
2. *Confidentiality*: ensures appropriate handling of confidential information
3. *Privacy*: controls for collecting, storing, and handling of personal information
4. *Processing Integrity*: controls error detection, fixing, and monitoring. Including accurate storage of information
5. *Availability*: controls for infrastructure availability and recovery procedures

Each of the TSCs contains a list of controls. There are numerous controls in the Common Criteria, including:

- Control Environment
- Communication and Information
- Risk Assessment
- Monitoring Activities
- Control Activities
- Logical and Physical Access Controls
- System Operations
- Change Management
- Risk Mitigation

The Committee of Sponsoring Organizations of the Treadway Commission, also known as COSO®, created a COSO framework[2] that goes hand in hand with the TSC.

There are five components of the COSO framework, and all are mapped to the TSC. All five COSO components and their 17 controls must be met to achieve the requirements of an SOC 2 report.

The 17 internal control principles from the COSO framework have been mapped into the Security/Common Criteria. COSO is mapped and covered by the first five controls in the Common Criteria as follows:

1. *Control Environment* covers COSO Principles 1–5, including the service organization's commitment to integrity and ethical values, management and independent board oversight, and the hiring, maintaining, and ongoing monitoring practices of employees.
2. *Communication and Information* covers COSO Principles 13–15, including the communication of relevant information to internal staff and clients of the service organization. Some examples of communication include lines of authority, boundaries of the system, and change management.
3. *Risk Assessment* covers COSO Principles 6–9, demonstrating that the service organization is assessing potential risks impacting their operations and establishing mitigation plans for these risks.
4. *Monitoring Activities* covers COSO Principles 16–17, including the ongoing monitoring of the system at the service organization and appropriate notification when there is a system breakdown.
5. *Control Activities* covers COSO Principles 10–12, including testing that the service organization has controls in place for risk mitigation, ensuring that these controls are monitored on an ongoing basis.

You can download the full SOC 2 criteria and its mapping to COSO on the AICPA website.[3]

A SOC 2 report is typically 30–100+ pages and consists of four sections.

1. *Independent Auditors Report*: audit opinion on the system description, design, and operating effectiveness to meet the control objectives, as per the scoped TSCs.
2. *Management Assertions*: assertions made by management that relate to the systems under audit. Note that these assertions are made directly by management and not the auditor. It should be treated as self-attested information.
3. *Description of the System*: an overview of the services/offering, including what the product/service is used for, transmitted/stored data, types of users, locations of staff, and other internal information.
4. *Auditor's Tests of Controls and Results of Test*: information about the controls, report objectives, testing methodology, and results.

Type 1 versus Type 2 SOC 2 Reports

There are two flavors of SOC 2 reports: type 1 and type 2. Essentially, Type 2 is a more robust report and often organizations start with Type 1, graduating to Type 2 due to time and cost considerations.

A Type 1 report focuses on the suitability of the design of controls and is a point in time. A Type 2 report goes a step further, assessing the operating effectiveness of controls over a specified time period.

Here are the key differences:

- A Type 1 report details the procedures and controls, while a Type 2 report evidences the operation of these controls over a time period.
- A Type 1 report attests to the suitability of the Service Organization controls, while a Type 2 report provides an opinion regarding the operating effectiveness of those controls over the specified period.
- A Type 1 report details procedures and controls as of a specific date, while a Type 2 report tests how the controls have been operating during a time period.
- A Type 1 report can be produced in about 8–12 weeks (2–6 weeks to draft, and then 2–6 weeks for the actual audit). A Type 2 report may take well over a year to produce (2–8 weeks to draft, 6 to 12 months to collect evidence with a sampling methodology over time, and 4 to 8 weeks for the audit.
- A Type 1 report can cost anywhere from $10k to $30k, whereas a Type 2 report can cost from $30k to $200k+ based on scope and provider.

How Is SOC 2 Report Relevant for Vendor Due Diligence Process

Since the SOC 2 report provides an independent opinion of the control environment, an assessor can rely on the report without having to review individual evidence directly. In case a SOC 2 Type 2 appropriately scoped report is available from a credible audit firm, it can accelerate the process, providing a win-win to both a vendor and a customer. Here are the key benefits:

- Independent: SOC 2 is independently attested, meaning it is not a self-declaration by the vendor

- *Time and Effort*: Time and effort of producing a SOC 2 report is exponentially greater than a typical vendor assessment, providing a deeper level of due diligence.
- *Access to Deeper Evidence than a Vendor Audit*: Evidence reviewed by an auditor who produced a SOC 2 report is deeper than what typically a customer would get access to during a vendor audit.
- *Sampling over a Time Period*: In the case of a Type 2 report testing was done over a time period, unlike a vendor audit that looks at controls as a point in time.

While an SOC 2 report may be helpful in the vendor due diligence process, there are numerous pitfalls in its use.

- *Product/Service Scope*: does the report cover the exact service you are using as a customer? That is by far the most significant pitfall. If your service uses a different control environment than the one covered in the report, you cannot be assured that the same controls are in place.
- *Coverage*: which of the 5 TSCs are included in the report, and are the missing TSCs relevant for the service you consume? Too often we see reports that only cover security and confidentiality, excluding privacy, processing integrity, and availability.
- *Audit Firm Reputation*: is audit firm well-recognized and reliable? Any AICPA-affiliated certified public accountant (CPA) can perform a SOC 2 audit. A key point of getting a SOC 2 report is to have someone independently vouch for your controls. A lot more weight is placed on a report from a Big 4 Audit firm vs a bargain-basement auditor. The more-known Audit firms typically command a higher premium due to their brand name.
- *Issue Date*: the SOC 2 report is good for a year, and a stale report is not a good representation of the control environment. Between SOC reports, audit firms may issue a "Bridge Letter" as an intermediate validation.
- *Significant Subservice Organizations*: does the report cover critical vendors (a.k.a subservice organization, or fourth parties)? It is important to understand which fourth parties are used and how the service organization manages these vendors. For example, if a Cloud service provider

is used behind the scenes, most of the security controls will be either shared or operated by the Cloud service provider. Look for a dedicated section called "Subservice organizations" or look for any references if subservice organizations were out of scope.

- *Complementary User Entity Controls*: these controls are disclosed to you as a customer. The vendor informs you that for their controls to operate effectively, there are specific things you must do as a customer in support of these controls. This section is optional, but there are at times more than a dozen controls disclosed. It is critical to understand which vendors have specific Complementary User Entity Controls disclosed and that you have taken steps on your side accordingly. Be ready for your Internal Audit team or regulators to see evidence that you are keeping track of this information.

- *Noted Exceptions*: if the auditor found any gaps in the control environment, then it will be disclosed as exceptions in the report. You should always review exceptions and determine if it is relevant for your consumption of the service. We saw cases where customers would get an SOC 2 report with an exception and not assess the impact of that exception.

Because of the sensitive details in the SOC 2 report, it is considered restricted and only shared per request with customers under confidentiality provisions (Figure 13.1).

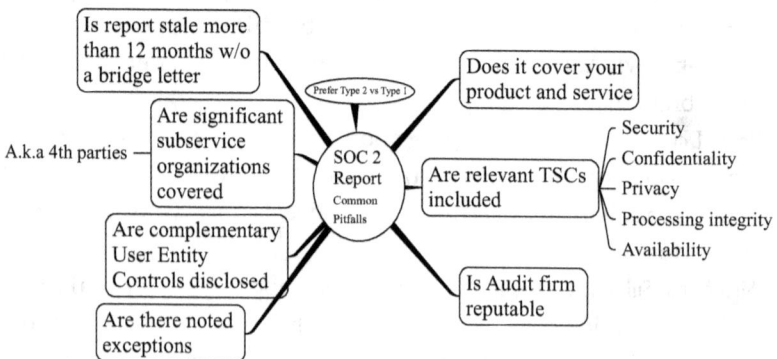

Figure 13.1 SOC2 Report Common Pitfalls

SOC 2 Reports Use in the Sales Process

Regardless of controversy surrounding its usefulness, a SOC 2 report is often a key part of the vendor due diligence process. Some customers may insist that not having one available will result in an extended level of due diligence, holding up deals or renewals.

A SOC 2 report is particularly important for startups or new products that sell to regulated industries such as Financial Services or Healthcare. Customers in these industries expect a greater level of due diligence and having a credible SOC 2 report often eases the process. Investment in an SOC 2 report demonstrates some commitment to risk management and provides a level of confidence for customers. At the same time, some customers completely disregard a SOC 2 report and exclusively rely on their specific questions and control assessment.

For larger enterprises, there are often dozens of individual SOC 2 reports due to fragmented products and services. As the intensity of vendor due diligence is increasing due to regulatory requirements, there is an increased use of industry-accepted vendor certifications such as SOC 2 reports. Sometimes investment in a SOC 2 report is also a marketing recommendation to improve brand equity and communicate a greater level of trust.

Unfortunately, there are still too many unsophisticated customers who blindly accept sub-par quality SOC 2 reports as a replacement for their vendor audit. While that is a poor form of risk management, it helps vendors to get deal revenue flowing and keep sales folks happy.

Notes

1   "SSAE16", Wikipedia.org, https://en.wikipedia.org/wiki/SSAE_16.
2   "Committee of Sponsoring Organizations of the Treadway Commission Enterprise Risk Management Integrating with Strategy and Performance",COSO.org, June 2017, https://www.coso.org/enterprise-risk-management.
3   "Mapping 2017 TSC", AICPA.org, https://us.aicpa.org/content/dam/aicpa/interestareas/frc/assuranceadvisoryservices/downloadabledocuments/othermapping/mapping-final-2017-tsc-to-extant-2016-tspc.xlsx.

PART III

BUILDING THE VENDOR CYBER RISK MANAGEMENT PROGRAM

14

PREPARATION

Executive Sponsorship and Key Stakeholders

Looking back at what makes most cybersecurity and TPRM programs successful, executive sponsorship is the single most important factor. It's all about tone from the top and appropriate organizational placement. At this point, cybersecurity management is well accepted across the industry and CISO is a common role in many enterprises. Vendor risk management is also getting traction, but often gets caught in turf wars in terms of ownership and functional reporting.

In practice, placement in CISO organizations is the most common if the focus is specifically for cybersecurity. In fact, CISO almost always has a key role in the overall program. That said, for larger enterprises, vendor risk management is typically recognized as a broader practice, with cybersecurity being one of multiple risk domains. There may be an overall TPRM program that is placed elsewhere within the organizational hierarchy, supported by CISO, CIO, or CTO for specific technical areas.

DOI: 10.4324/9781003581321-17

Ability to understand key stakeholders, organizational goals, and ultimately, executive sponsorship differentiates success from failure. There is not a one size fits all approach, and it is essential to be flexible over time. A governance structure that includes a steering committee chaired by a senior executive is often an effective approach.

A good initial diagnostic set of five questions as you are forming the program includes:

1. Does my manager understand why this program needs to be formed and what are the key objectives?
2. Does my manager's overall responsibility align with the key objectives of the program?
3. Who are all the other key stakeholders across the enterprise and how will they support this program?
4. How does cybersecurity risk fit into the overall enterprise risk framework?
5. How are top management of the company and the Board engaged and informed of the program?

Asking these questions upfront leads to effective conversations on how your program will be supported, reduce organizational friction, and avoid potential territorial friction. It is important to consider stakeholders' engagement through every phase of the lifecycle (Figure 14.1).

Figure 14.1 Organizational Placement

Alignment with Risk Appetite and Enterprise Risk Framework

In the executive sponsorship section, we introduced alignment with the enterprise risk framework as one of the key diagnostic questions. It is important to realize that cybersecurity and risk management are accountability of the Board and top company management. CISO, CIO, and CRO are not responsible for making decisions on accepting risks, but instead only responsible for ensuring risks are appropriately represented and governance framework is in place to manage these risks. For many medium and large enterprises, there is an enterprise risk framework in place that articulates an overall risk appetite, appropriate limits, and ways to measure key risk indicators aligned to those limits. Within every enterprise risk framework there are risk stripes that typically address operational risk, and in turn, within operational risk there is cybersecurity and third-party risk. If an enterprise risk framework already exists, then it is essential that your program is aligned within that overall structure. Not accounting for that structure has a substantial risk of organizational misalignment and management expectations mismatch, which is rarely a career enhancer.

Based on industry and company size, an enterprise risk framework may not be in place. In those cases, it is advisable to determine governance that ensures top management visibility and decision making for issues that your program will be raising.

Key Objectives

We discussed in earlier chapters regulatory velocity for vendor risk, and compliance with multitude regulations is certainly a key objective of any cyber vendor risk program. That said, a compliance-focused program will often be behind the curve, and instead it is helpful to think about managing risk as the primary focus. Often the two objectives overlap, with examples of data privacy requirements for vendors that have access to your sensitive information or ensuring the use of dual-factor authentication for your vendor products. In other cases, risk reduction is not directly aligned with regulatory requirements. For example, by eliminating privileged access from your high-risk contractors, while not a compliance requirement, it is one of the meaningful ways to reduce risk in your overall vendor portfolio.

Additional objectives may include improving the time to market to introduce new products and services or overall cost-effectiveness.

Vendor Inventory

In planning a vendor cyber risk management program, having an initial understanding of size is driven by having a vendor inventory. Surprisingly, an accurate inventory of vendors, and their associated products and services often does not exist. For initial sizing, an inventory will help you right-size your program. The following dimensions should be considered.

- Estimated count of vendors
- Estimated count of associated vendor services
- Initial modelling of vendors that fall into High-Medium-Low category based on inherent risk. In a subsequent chapter, we will discuss in more detail how to determine inherent risk, but at this point any initial indication will suffice. Typically, high risk is reserved for vendors that have access to your confidential data or provide a critical business service.
- Clarification if company inter-affiliates are in scope of your program, and if so associated count of inter-affiliates.
- Clarification if fourth parties are in scope, and if so an associated count.

Surprisingly, getting access to this information is often challenging. You may have to work with IT Asset Management and Procurement teams to review the payable history and conduct a series of interviews to compile initial vendor lists. If an inventory already exists, it will be helpful to pressure-test data quality by reviewing with key stakeholders. A common blind spot includes shadow IT, where business areas leverage SaaS or Cloud solutions without IT involvement.

Lack of a reliable inventory or material data quality issues should be prioritized for remediation as part of the program.

Key Personnel and Consultants

Typically, there is a sense of urgency to get started, but there is only one problem - you need qualified help to get the job done. There are two types of resources you will need:

- Someone with institutional knowledge who can help you navigate internally.
- Domain experts with a depth of experience in cybersecurity and specifically vendor risk management.

It is critical to secure institutional knowledge as either a dedicated resource(s) or, at a minimum, access to help when you need it. Every enterprise is unique, and without a trusted advisor who knows where the light switches are, it is easy to get lost.

Longer term domain expertise is often better suited as permanent hires but help from experienced consultants is frequently an effective way to get started or to augment capacity. Complete reliance on external expertise without in-house domain knowledge would likely result in a sub-optimized and expensive outcome. Similarly, not getting access to external expertise may slow down your progress, may limit your access to ongoing industry best practices, and may hamper your ability to react to peaks and valleys.

Consulting help can come in multiple shapes and sizes:

- Staff augmentation from a consulting firm
- A boutique firm specializing in this space
- Individual contractor(s) with relevant experience
- Outcome-based managed service solution that may optionally come with bundled tooling

Based on the required scale and funding availability the best solution may vary.

Most of the Big 4 consulting firms offer a full range of third-party risk services. For example, Ernst & Young (EY) offers evaluation, risk monitoring, and risk identification services.[1]

A managed service option is an increasingly popular choice that can provide sustainable help and hold your partner accountable. RiskQ[2] provides a third-party managed service for supply chain risk.

Tooling

An Excel spreadsheet and macros are not tools to run a vendor risk program of any size. An essential part of the planning process is to consider a software solution to support your immediate and future needs. Vendor risk management is a crowded market with GRC solutions, specialized vendor management solutions, a collection of specific tools, some with managed services options.

Some solutions specifically target cybersecurity vendor risk needs, some target broader TPRM lifecycle, some are more sourcing focused, and some are primarily enterprise risk management oriented. As we discussed earlier, it is important to recognize if there is an enterprise risk management framework, and if so if it is supported by an established GRC tool. One option could be to extend GRC functionality to satisfy the needs of your specific program.

A common mistake is to select a tool without considering implementation and maintenance costs, which often dwarf the actual licensing fees. GRCs typically require working with experienced implementation partners for professional services, an expensive and prolonged value proposition. Solutions like RiskQ's TRPM are inexpensive and allow the company to manage supply chain risk on their own.

Funding

Now that you have confirmed executive sponsorship, got a sense of your vendor inventory, and understood resource and tooling requirements, it is time to put your sponsor(s) to work and ensure that you have adequate funding in support of your program. It is your responsibility to articulate funding needs for the program and actively advocate for adequate funding support. Getting funding is not a one and done, but an ongoing conversation as your program matures. Having an outcome-based and risk-based conversation is essential to explain to your sponsor what you need to be successful. For example, explaining specific control environment weaknesses and your plan to mitigate that gap will be a productive way to demonstrate the need for funding.

Objective criteria, such as industry benchmarking, or proposals from third-party/management consulting firms can help to shape your estimates. It is important to consider staffing, software, and any additional requirements as part of your estimate.

In larger companies, getting funding requires the ability to navigate internal processes, and at times a bit of internal salesmanship.

Strategic Roadmap

It is never too early to develop a strategic roadmap, demonstrating how vendor cyber risk management capability is going to evolve over time. A key to a successful roadmap is to define objectives that resonate with your leadership and your specific organization. There are several approaches that you may take. Here are some options that work well in practice:

- A popular approach can include defining program phases, with key objectives for each phase.
- Maturity assessments are common for defining a framework. Shared Assessments published a five-level maturity model for vendor risk management that goes from initial visioning to continuous improvement.[3]
- Another successful approach is to define control gaps across either risk domains or phases of the life cycle. The roadmap can demonstrate how these gaps are addressed with each phase of the program.
- An assessment against an industry framework such as NIST, or a blended framework, can demonstrate how key domains will mature over each phase of the program. That approach enables prioritization of specific control areas.
- If there is an enterprise risk framework, alignment with risk appetite and limits is an effective way of measuring adoption. You may define specific KPIs as your risk tolerance. For example, ensure 0% privileged access to third parties.

The roadmap may be milestone-based, where you set a goal for specific accomplishments in your project plan. Some accomplishments may include getting to certain levels of maturity for popular cybersecurity rating providers such as SecurityScorecard™, BitSight™, or MasterCard RiskRecon™. In many cases, the initial roadmap should be drafted in the early stages and act as a baseline to be refined over time.

Regardless of what approach you take, remember that it is a multi-year journey, and a roadmap is a tool to communicate your vision and progress to key stakeholders.

Notes

1   "Third-party risk management services", EY, https://www.ey.com/en_us/
consulting/third-party-risk-management-consulting-services.
2   RiskQ, https://risk-q.com.
3   "VENDOR RISK MANAGEMENT MATURITY MODEL (VRMMM)", Shared
Assessments, https://sharedassessments.org/blog/a-roadmap-for-maturity-revving-
up-risk-management/.

15

DUE DILIGENCE

Terms to Include in Vendor Contracts

A key aspect of effectively managing third parties is establishing fit-for-purpose contractual minimum requirements within a contract template. It is important to align these contractual terms for any new vendor engagements and establish a remediation program to look back into existing contracts where these terms are missing.

Our guidance is to ask the vendor to follow your security requirements so that they align as nearly as possible. Considering that, here are the Top 10 contractual considerations:

1. *Audit Rights*: should be required for any high-risk vendor. It is important to obtain annual audit rights. The audit rights include onsite or comprehensive due diligence obligations. Consideration includes provisions for a subcontractor or a third-party assessment vendor to perform this work on your behalf. In some cases, the vendor may insist that you pay for their time to support these audits.

DOI: 10.4324/9781003581321-18

2. *Data Protection*: should be required for any vendor that will handle your sensitive data. It is essential to define data security provisions and align them to any vendor obligations for handling that data. The contract should define the vendor's obligations for appropriately protecting your data according to information security best practices in combination with legal & regulatory requirements based on relevant jurisdictions. In cases where the third party is also a competitor for some part of their business, you may want to request further segregation requirements from people, data, and process perspective.

3. *Code Escrow*: should be required for any technology vendor that is providing software supporting your critical business services.

4. *Client Service Provisions*: should be considered if a third party supports your customers by providing you services related to client inquiries. All customer complaints need to be relayed and handled with proper care.

5. *Incident Management*: should be required to define contractual obligations that outline how you will be notified in case of a cyber incident or data breach that impacts your data and levels of service.

6. *Change Management*: should be considered based on the type of service you receive and its importance. This includes defining how you need to be informed regarding changes and what rights you must participate in a third party's change management process.

7. *Liability Limits*: should be considered in the case where a third party may mishandle your data or IP and you may sue. This includes the negotiation of liability limits. In reverse, in cases where your firm may mishandle third-party data or IP which may cause an issue that results in a lawsuit, it is important to negotiate your liability limits as low as possible.

8. *Notifications of Critical 4th Parties and Cloud Services*: should be considered in cases where your third party decides to subcontract the work to another party. You should always be contacted with sufficient notices and ideally have a say in ongoing decision-making. In cases where your critical third party is providing cloud services; you likely will have regulatory obligations to have a risk treatment strategy. In all cases, it is essential that the obligations of a third party carry through to the rest of their supply chain as much as practical.

9. *Antivirus and Malware*: should be required by your third parties to take commercially reasonable measures to ensure that all data that is sent to you is virus and malware free.

10. *Non-Disclosure Agreements (NDAs)*: It is a best practice to use NDAs before a contract is signed to protect IP and other considerations as commercial discussions take place. Appropriate NDA terms should be incorporated into each contract based on a type of service received.

Two Spectrums of Control Environment Transparency

In an ideal world of full transparency, unlimited time, and resources we would want every company to ensure that the control environment of each vendor they use is completely aligned with their own policies, and procedures. Additionally, Operational Risk (Line two) and Internal Audit (Line three) teams would review all internal procedures and underlying infrastructure behind every vendor software product.

In a perfect world, we want to have the same information for every software product licensed by a third party evaluated consistently. Having a solid baseline to compare vendor-developed software to in-house software makes it easier to assess vendor products.

On the opposite end of the spectrum, we use outsourcing to leverage vendor capability and get the business outcomes we require without having to worry about the "how." Software and Business Process Outsourcing are typically bundled together as a Managed Service that only gives you visibility of the output, leaving the vendor to deal with all the nuts and bolts. Understanding if your software is end of life (EOL) is a basic requirement for your cybersecurity program. Those same requirements should be applied to the third party who builds your software.

In the United States, prior to Office of Control of Currency (OCC) 2013 Third-Party Relationships risk management guidance,[1] that mandate was not clear. It continues to be clarified by multiple global regulators, including the OCC 2020 supplement,[2] and Third-Party Relationships Interagency Guidance on Risk Management.[3] This demonstrates a continued shift to the left, moving from an arm's length black box approach to a more accountable approach that allows for a better understanding of the control environments of your vendors.

Risk-based Treatment Strategy

Despite the shift to the left, it is physically impossible to do full due diligence on every vendor that your enterprise uses. Some vendors, for example, such as a local print shop do not require the same level of due diligence as your cloud provider.

In prior chapters we spoke about developing a vendor inventory, classifying each vendor product/service based on inherent risk. Inherent risk is typically driven by questions such as:

- Does the vendor have access to my confidential data, or personal data of my customers, critical third parties, etc.?
- Does the vendor provide a critical service that would interrupt my business beyond my risk tolerance?
- How much data is my cloud service processing?

A well-designed, inherent risk profile typically consists of 3–20 questions that measure the level of inherent risk proportionately using a scale of Low/Medium/High, or the CMMI approach of zero to five. Designing the right amount of information needed to evaluate the vendor should be based on the context of what the vendor does. We have seen inherent risk models based on 100+ questions with carefully calibrated weight averages resulting in a scale of 1–100, or a simple methodology with three questions, resulting in a three-category risk rating. At times, unnecessary sophistication of modeling and numerical precision gives an illusion of a better outcome. There are three principles to keep in mind when designing the vendor inherent risk model:

1. Employees who are responsible for these vendor relationships across your enterprise are not likely risk management professionals or dedicated to that role. It is more likely something they do on the side. Therefore, simplicity and lack of ambiguity in questions are key.
2. The ultimate outcome of a typical distribution of inherent risk ratings should demonstrate most of the risks as low, and the minority of the risks as high.
   - Low: 50–70%
   - Medium: 20–30%
   - High or Critical: 5–20%

Table 15.1 Due Diligence Frequency Table

Inherent Risk Rating	Due Diligence Type	Frequency
Low	Compliance screening and cybersecurity rating provider monitoring	At onboarding, and when there is a significant change
Medium	Remote assessment	At onboarding, when there is a significant change, or every three years
High	Onsite assessment	At onboarding, when there is a significant change, or every year

3. Any time you look to change an inherent risk model, back-test the impact on your current vendor inventory to estimate what the expected impact will be. That should be done by sampling the current population and assessing projected estimates in terms of volumes and potential costs.

Based on the inherent risk rating, there should be a predetermined due diligence treatment strategy that is specified by type and duration. For example, a common framework may include something like Table 15.1.

You will notice that at onboarding there is normally an expected level of due diligence. That is typically a good opportunity to incorporate due diligence as part of the actual sourcing decision and use it as a criterion to compare multiple vendors. That is also the time where you will get more collaboration from the vendor to work with you, accommodating any requests for greater transparency. After all, there is a revenue opportunity for them at stake. At the time of onboarding, you likely will get the most pressure from internal business stakeholders to get quickly through the due diligence process since it may impact project timelines or business value realization.

Another salient point is that due diligence should be performed not just at a predetermined frequency, but also when there is a meaningful change. That is easier said than done. You need to have mature processes to be informed of what defines when the vendor service that is consumed changes, or if there is a change on the vendor side in how they provide a service. It also requires contractual change management notification requirements and service level agreements (SLAs) to be specifically informed of such changes. It is important to define as per your processes and procedures when there is a material change in the vendor services.

Designing the Due Diligence Questionnaire

A key part of the vendor due diligence process is designing an effective questionnaire (Figure 15.1). Typically, a questionnaire is sent to a vendor as part of the RFP process, onboarding process, or ongoing vendor due diligence cycle.

The vendor questionnaire needs to align to your key controls that in turn align to your vendor cybersecurity policy. To determine what questions should be included in your questionnaire you should work backwards from your cybersecurity vendor policy.

The vendor cybersecurity policy is specific to your enterprise. It should be based on an industry framework such as ISO 27001, NIST, etc. It should be aligned with your compliance risk management by mapping key regulations.

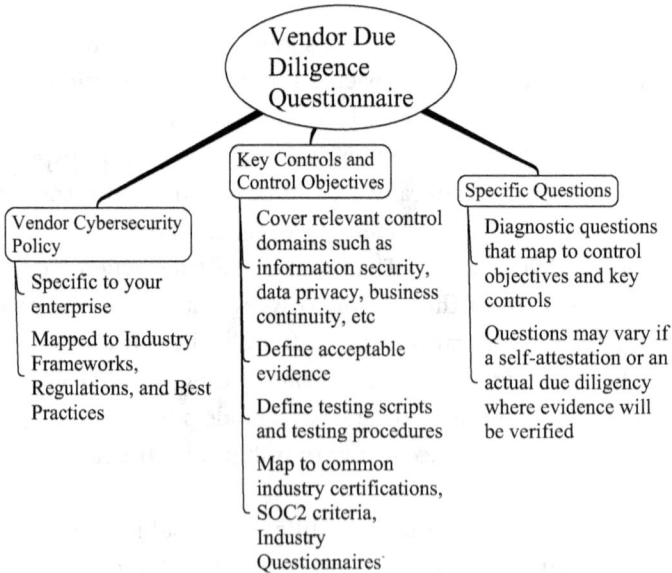

Figure 15.1 Vendor Due Diligence Questionnaire

Based on your policy, you should map relevant key controls and control objectives that be included in your vendor due diligence. These control objectives should cover relevant control domains such as information security, data privacy, business continuity, etc. Determine which operating procedures, acceptable evidence, and testing scripts are needed for each control objective. Consider upfront how these control objectives map to popular certifications or popular industry questionnaires.

Finally, for each control objective, determine a set of diagnostic questions that would effectively capture desired information. Please note that if questionnaires are used for self-attestation, the questions need to be either yes/no or multiple choice. If this questionnaire is used for verification of evidence, then the question can be more open ended and should request the actual evidence.

A common mistake is to have questionnaires that ask too many questions, or request evidence that is not in the correct context or will not be reviewed internally. The goal should be to have a concise number of questions to get the minimum viable information needed. Having unnecessary information is not only burdensome for your vendors, but it also slows down the process and makes you potentially liable by having information that you did not review in case of a cyber insurance claim related to a vendor breach. Not all vendors will be willing to share their sensitive internal documents with their customers as that may expose them to security risks and can be against their information security policy. Requesting information that most vendors refuse to provide results in frustration, cost, and delays on both sides.

Another common mistake is sending a full set of questions to every vendor without scoping considerations based on vendor type and how you consume specific vendor service. For example, if a vendor does not have access to your sensitive data, then it is wasteful to ask questions about data privacy. A typical due diligence questionnaire request should not be more than 100–200 questions.

In prior chapters, we reviewed best practices of leveraging SOC reports and other vendor certifications as part of your due diligence process. It is important to appropriately rely on common vendor certifications, but that by itself does not fully replace your due diligence.

Many vendors, when asked for due diligence questions, share a SIG by Shared Assessments.[4] SIG consists of a set of standardized questions across numerous control domains that vendors share with customers. It is a useful source of information if you are looking for self-attested responses. It is worth the effort to map the SIG questions to your process to avoid unnecessary back and forth. SIG is typically updated annually, and the mapping should include the latest and prior year's version.

Another emerging approach is to work with industry-shared assessment utilities, such as S&P Global KY3P, VenMinder, and ProcessUnity. Each of the utilities has its specific framework. Similar to SIG if you decide to work with one or more of these utilities then it is important to map your questions to their framework.

Issues Management and Remediation

There is not much point in performing due diligence without expecting issues to be discovered and developing a robust process to deal with resulting issues. Some questions to be ready for:

- Are you ready to terminate a vendor relationship if an important cybersecurity issue is not remediated by your vendor?
- Who has appropriate decision rights to accept resulting issues?
- Are you able to put compensating controls if there is a control gap on the vendor side?
- How long will you give a vendor to remediate discovered issues, and do you have contractual rights to demand action?
- Do you have the commercial leverage to insist on issue remediation (perhaps a new pending deal or a major renewal coming up)?

There are four common dispositions for discovered issues:

1. Accept the risk by authorized parties based on risk limits and risk taxonomy. For example, you may have a process that allows medium risk to be accepted by a senior director, where high risk to be accepted by CEO with an approved plan for compensating controls.
2. Remediate risk by the vendor within specified duration. Typically based on risk level standard remediation period can be predetermined. For example, lack of dual-factor authentication can be considered high risk and to be remediated within three months.

3. Collaboratively remediate the risk with the vendor and internal stakeholders. For example, a dedicated networking connection between the vendor and your office requires provisioning on both sides.
4. Terminate the vendor relationship and trigger an exit strategy. In case there is not a viable option for timely remediation, you may have no choice but to terminate the contract. It is important to have appropriate plans in place to switch to another vendor or internal solution that mitigates business disruption.

Tying Due Diligence in Vendor Life Cycle

Due diligence process is a cornerstone of a vendor life cycle and does not exist in isolation. Starting from a solid contractual framework that is applied to every vendor relationship and ending with governance framework to deal with resulting issues.

As the regulatory environment continues to evolve to demand greater transparency and accountability of vendor relationships, the due diligence process should continue to be refined to remain fit-for-purpose.

Notes

1   Office of the Controller of the Currency (2013, October 30). Third-party relationships: Risk management guidance. https://www2.occ.gov/news-issuances/news-releases/2013/nr-occ-2013-167.html.
2   Office of the Controller of the Currency. (2020). Third-party relationships: Frequently asked questions to supplement OCC Bulletin 2013–29. https://www2.occ.gov/news-issuances/news-releases/2013/nr-occ-2013-167.html.
3   Office of the Controller of the Currency (2023, June 6). Third-party relationships interagency guidance on risk management. https://www2.occ.gov/news-issuances/bulletins/2023/bulletin-2023-17.html.
4   Shared Assessments. Standardized information gathering questionnaire. https://sharedassessments.org/sig/.

16

RISK ASSESSMENTS

Strategy to Access Your Vendor Risk

Vendor risk assessment has been a breeding ground of exciting innovation, challenging many preconceived notions. With enterprise vendor portfolios often shape-shifting and not well understood, it is helpful to have a holistic approach to decipher signal through the noise.

Assessing vendor risk is both a best practice and a regulatory expectation by global regulators. It is essential that compliance obligations are understood and incorporated as part of the vendor risk assessment process.

In prior chapters we spoke about developing a vendor inventory, classifying each vendor product/service based on inherent risk, methodology to classify vendors based on inherent risk, and developing a risk treatment strategy for vendor due diligence. Vendor inventory, inherent risk classification, and vendor due diligence have been the bread and butter of vendor risk management programs. It is a fundamental foundation of a vendor risk assessment strategy.

DOI: 10.4324/9781003581321-19

Overall, vendor portfolio assessment is typically the right place to start, relying initially on inherent risk classifications. More targeted vendor due diligence can go as deep as onsite assessments, or as lite-touch as self-attestations based on a vendor questionnaire. Resulting from vendor due diligence is a list of residual risks (risks that do not have adequate compensating controls), that is considered as part of the overall vendor portfolio assessment.

As an alternative to interacting with each vendor, there are numerous approaches that can augment traditional due diligence by looking outside-in. These assessments can either be done at a portfolio level or for individual vendors.

In addition to assessing your immediate third parties, an assessment can include a deeper dive within your supply chain, including 4th and "Nth" parties.

More specialized assessments can include an analysis of Bill of Material for either hardware or software components used across your application or hardware inventory. That can apply to either commercial or open-source software.

As all these techniques combine, there is a bridge between point-in-time assessments and continuous monitoring that is an essential part of your overall process. That can include threat intelligence, negative news monitoring, and scores from cybersecurity rating providers.

There is also a need to assess and monitor specific vendor SLAs and vendor compliance with contractual obligations. Some of these SLAs are technical and should be considered as part of the assessment process (Figure 16.1).

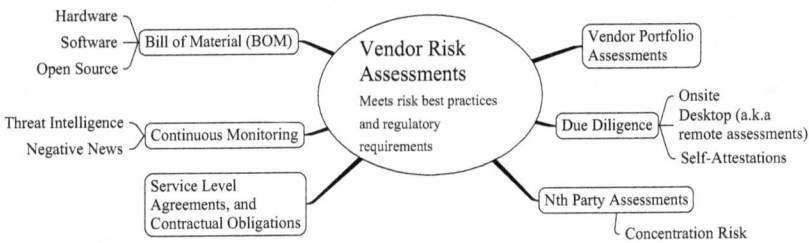

Figure 16.1 Vendor Risk Assessments Best Practices

Onsite Assessments

The holy grail of vendor risk assessments for years has been onsite assessments. As per the prior chapter, that is typically reserved for high-risk or critical vendors and lets you sort of look under the hood and look the vendor's CISO in the eye to see if they have anything to hide. Common characteristics of onsite assessments include:

- A one-day or multi-day visit to one or more physical locations.
- Preceded by preparation work of getting preliminary responses from a vendor to a questionnaire and identifying specific areas of focus. That enables the vendor to identify appropriate individuals.
- Getting access to internal documents or a series of interviews, screen shares, and process walkthroughs that otherwise may be considered too sensitive to share outside of physical walls.
- Going beyond control design assessment, and testing control effectiveness for certain controls by looking at small samples. Sample of one is common, unlike a SOC report that looks for a much larger sample and over a period of time.
- Performing physical security review, by looking at data centers, physical access controls, and potentially health and safety.

For larger vendors, there is typically a dedicated team focused on accommodating customer requests for onsite assessments. Due to the sensitivity of shared information, customer relationship management component, and expense of hosting onsite visits, there is normally a level of effort to discourage customers from requesting these onsite visits. That discouragement can come in the form of requiring a contractual clause of a periodic vendor audit, requiring customers to pay for onsite assessments, scheduling delays, or in some cases refusal to accommodate. In some cases, vendors make a robust evidence inventory available to their customers, where access is only physically allowed onsite, forcing customers to take time and expense.

COVID-19 pandemic added an interesting twist to onsite assessments. How do you do onsite assessments when offices are closed, and travel is prohibited? The industry tried to adapt on both customers and vendor sides.

- There has been increased willingness by vendor CISOs to screen share more sensitive information that previously was only available onsite.

- Some customers have extended the scope and depth of their desktop (also known as remote) assessment to test deeper.
- Some customers tweaked their policies to reduce frequency of onsite assessments or secured risk acceptance during the pandemic.
- Creative approaches emerged such as specialized screen sharing tools that prevent screen capture, or CCTV footage of data centers that can serve as evidence of physical security.

The unfortunate reality is that there is a false perception that onsite assessments always add an increased level of assurance for vendor controls. Too often these assessments are outsourced and turned into a check-the-box exercise. The depth and quality of onsite assessments can vary. There are often risk policies that are not fit for purpose, mandating annual onsite assessments for high-risk vendors, making it virtually impossible to comply with such requirements.

Desktop (also known as Remote) Assessments

A bread and butter of vendor risk assessment programs are the desktop assessments. Like onsite assessments, depth and quality can greatly vary. In many cases desktop assessments can be more robust than onsite assessments.

Common characteristics of desktop assessments include:

- A one-day or multi-day series of screen-sharing sessions or phone interviews, preceded by preparation work, of getting preliminary responses from a vendor to a questionnaire and identifying specific areas of focus. That enables the vendor to identify appropriate individuals.
- Getting access to internal documents or a series of interviews, screen shares, and process walkthroughs that were deemed to be not too sensitive to share outside of physical walls.
- Typically limited to control design assessment, and not actually testing control effectiveness by looking at small samples. In cases of control effectiveness, a sample of one is most common, unlike a SOC report that looks for a much larger sample and over a period of time.
- Typically excluding actual physical security reviews but may review policies and procedures for physical reviews.

Self-Attestations

Some may consider self-attestations as a form of vendor due diligence. It is important to be deliberate upfront in what controls self-attestation is sufficient for, vs. actual verification of evidence. For example, a question of "Do you have an Information Security Policy Y/N?" is considered a self-attestation. Alternatively, "Do you have an Information Security Policy Y/N? and please attach if applicable" is not a self-attestation. As a best practice, all documents provided should be reviewed for completeness, consistency, and expected minimum requirements. Asking for documents and then failing to review them is not only wasteful but exposes you to liability in case of a cyber insurance claim.

Typically, some self-attestation questions can be included as part of a desktop assessment and may guide more targeted follow-ups if appropriate. An assessment that is mostly based on self-attestations offers limited value and can be used for lower risk vendors.

Alternative Assessment Approaches and Continuous Monitoring

Not all assessments require vendor interactions, and there are an increasing number of effective approaches without any vendor engagement.

- Many vendors offer robust pages dedicated to demonstrating answers to their security questions, relevant certifications and attestations, and redacted security policies. Google Cloud™ is an excellent example of being proactive with their transparency.[1]
- Cybersecurity Rating providers such as SecurityScorecard use the FAIR™ method, BitSight uses an external scan to score threats, and RiskQ's ValuRisQ™ uses a digital scan to offer comprehensive reports on millions of companies based on monitoring numerous risk vectors. These ratings are not a good substitute for actual due diligence, but a good supplement that can be part of a fit-for-purpose approach. It can work especially well for lower risk vendors. The ratings in isolation do not take into consideration unique aspects of how specific vendor service is consumed, and therefore cannot appropriately calculate inherent and residual risk.

- Statistical approaches by pinpointing vendors with highest risks of data security breaches.[2] This approach uses publicly available information collected in a proprietary way, but like the weakness of the cybersecurity ratings approach, when used in isolation, does not address residual risk.

As some of these alternative approaches evolved beyond questionnaires and document reviews, the industry is increasing its reliance on data and continuous monitoring. Best of class cybersecurity vendor risk programs include continuous monitoring that is an essential part of the overall process. That can include threat intelligence, negative news monitoring, and scores from cybersecurity rating providers monitored daily.

Some very innovative software like RiskQ's ValuRisQ provides continuous control monitoring of MFA, open shares, patches, versions, permissions, and a host of controls.

Fourth and "Nth" Party Assessments

Supply chain risk is not limited to just immediate third parties. It is important to understand key fourth and "Nth" parties that you rely on. A starting point is to develop an inventory of key "Nth" parties as a combination approach of understanding your contracts, interviewing key internal stakeholders, and potentially reaching out to your vendors.

Subsequently, it is important to recognize that, in most cases, your fourth parties will not be open to vendor due diligence process as they do not have a direct contractual relationship with you. Alternative approaches outlined in section above are a good fit for Nth party assessments. Additional options may include working with industry-shared assessment utilities such as RiskQ ValuRisQ, S&P Global KY3P, VenMinder, and ProcessUnity to see what assessments are available off the shelf for these vendors. Please see Chapter 12 for further discussion on how to work with Shared Assessment utilities.

An effective "Nth" party assessment approach provides better visibility for overall vendor concentration risk across the entire supply chain and makes your program more reactive to industry breaches and service disruptions.

Notes

1   "Compliance offerings", *Google Cloud*, https://cloud.google.com/security/compliance/offerings.
2   Hann, D., & Lee, T. (2021, December 14). How to improve third-party risk management using statistical models. DHann Consulting and VivoSecurity. https://www.vivosecurity.com/_files/ugd/fc4221_5aacff2a3e964683b25ad77da07518a0.pdf.

17

VENDOR RISK QUANTIFICATION

Quantification of a Data Breach of a Third Party

When a third party is responsible for not protecting your data in a cloud service, you will pay to notify people of the breach. That cost ranges from US$10 to US$432 per individual record based on your industry.

Example of Third-Party Data Breach Losses

In the case of target, they paid out at a minimum US$400m in data exfiltration costs (40m records * US$10 a record) and US$18.5m in lawsuits. A phishing email sent to employees at Fazio Mechanical, who was target's third-party HVAC vendor delivered a "Citadel" Trojan malware. Fazio Mechanical's vendor credentials were stolen by attackers and used to access target's network. Attackers then exploited a web application vulnerability with an SQL injection method of attack. Once the backdoor was created, the attackers took their time conducting reconnaissance to locate the servers they wanted to steal data from. After the servers were located the

DOI: 10.4324/9781003581321-20

attackers probably used a "pass-the-hash" attack to steal an Admin access token to use to create a new Admin account. Next 70 million customers PII was stolen, but the servers did not store credit card #'s or associated info so attackers had to go after point-of-sale (POS) machines. Attackers next installed malware onto POS machines to copy all credit and debit card data used for purchases. After copying the data from the POS, the data was then forwarded to servers in America and Brazil to wait for the attackers to retrieve it at their convenience.

Best Practices to Minimize Data Breach Risk

Records that are archived offline or purged cannot be stolen. Having robust Information Lifecycle Management hygiene in place with your third parties will help to guarantee your data sources are being properly managed.

Quantification of a Business Interruption

Business interruption losses are based on the revenue lost, the costs to restore the systems, and fines and penalties due to unavailability.

Example of Third-Party Business Interruption Losses

Merck was among companies worldwide that were hit by the June 27, 2017, attack. NotPetya worked by infiltrating Microsoft systems that had not installed a needed security patch. It encrypted a user's data and sent a ransom message in order for users to take back control – although the ransom was actually a spoof, there was no real way for users to retrieve their data. It also had a worm-like capability that allowed it to spread across affected networks.

The company told its 70,000 employees on Tuesday to immediately cease all interactions with company networks, to refrain from turning on or rebooting any company computers or tablets, and to not use thumb drives. As company email was completely disabled, Merck supervisors disseminated instructions down the corporate ladder via copied and pasted text messages. The company did assure employees that human resource data had not been compromised.

It's unclear how Merck was infected with Petya, which partly relies on Eternal Blue, the leaked tool released by the mysterious hacker group Shadow Brokers and believed to be developed by the National Security Agency. While the majority of Merck employees are in the United States, the company has a worldwide presence, including an office in Ukraine.

Merck's plummeting productivity is hardly unique among Petya victims, and it's clear the ransomware has caused a significant drop in productivity around the globe. Ukrainian government workers have said they're reduced to only working via their smartphones. And on Wednesday, a representative for Maersk, the world's largest shipping company, said that the company had temporarily ceased taking any new orders.

Since the attack, Merck has instructed its US employees, largely comprised of a sales force scattered across the country, to run a low-fi operation. Employees have been communicating with clients exclusively via telephone and in-person meetings, along with keeping a paper record of their workdays. Those who work from regional offices and the company's New Jersey headquarters are told to refrain from connecting to company wifi.

As a partial fix, the company has created a makeshift temporary email server, accessible only via web browser, where employees can set up a new account to at least send and receive emails with a Merck domain via their personal computers. That doesn't give them access to old emails, though, and other functions, like Outlook calendar, aren't accessible. The company hopes to merge the email accounts once the original email network is restored.

It crippled Merck's in-house API manufacturing and affected its formulation and packaging systems, as well as R&D and other operations. The company said the attack had a US$260 million impact on sales, US$330 million impact on marketing and administrative expenses and production costs, and a US$200 million impact on 2018 sales through residual backlog. Most operations were restored within six months.

On top of that production of one of its best-selling products affected even as demand was growing. That forced Merck to borrow US240 million worth of Gardasil doses from the stockpile of the Center for Disease Control (CDC) due to the "temporary production shutdown resulting from the cyberattack, as well as overall higher demand than originally planned."

Merck has said that it cost US$125 million through a reduction in sales because of its inability to meet demand for Gardasil 9.

Best Practices to Minimize Business Interruption Loss

Have a strategy in place to restore your systems that includes the IT asset inventory of all the source and target data sources, critical business processes and systems. Use that as the plan to restore them. In addition,

- Backup your data at least once per day to an external hard drive or cloud.
- Always keep your operating system, web browsers, antivirus, and any other software updated to the latest version available.
- Use antivirus and firewalls.
- Use network segmentation to limit the spread as much as possible in the event of an attack. This will isolate the ransomware and prevent it from spreading to other systems.
- Use email protection against phishing attacks, which are the leading cause of malware infections.
- Use endpoint security that includes antivirus and anti-malware detection, data encryption, data loss prevention, intrusion detection, web browser security, mobile & desktop security, network assessments for security teams and real-time security alerts and notifications.
- Limit user access privileges. Least privilege typically involves a zero-trust model that assumes any internal or external users cannot be trusted, which means that they will require identity verification at every level of access. Verification requires at least two-factor authentication (2FA) or multi-factor authentication (MFA).
- Run regular security testing and implement new security measures.
- Use security awareness training including phishing, secure VPN use, privacy, and incident response.

18

THE ROLE OF POLICY AND PROCEDURE

Definition of Policy and Procedure

Policies and procedures are necessary to ensure consistency in an organization's operation. They must provide clarity and guidance in dealing with matters and activities that are central to the organization's functioning, such as health and safety, risk management, regulatory requirements, or issues that may have more severe consequences. According to the *Cambridge Dictionary*:

Policy[1] is "a set of ideas or a plan of what to do in particular situations that has been agreed to officially by a group of people, a business organization, a government, or a political party."

Procedure[2] is "a set of actions that is the official or accepted way of doing something."

DOI: 10.4324/9781003581321-21

The Distinction between Policy and Procedure

Any policy must be supported by appropriate procedures to make it effective. It is important to distinguish between them even though they must work in tandem to deliver diverse benefits.

Policies are general in nature, spell out the organization's position about various issues and provide rules and guidelines which help in decision-making consistent with their objectives.

Procedures are a description of specific activities and actions, alternative courses of actions, emergency processes and methods, and means to be deployed.

Policies and procedures empower employees and managers to clearly understand individual, team responsibilities, save time, and direct resources toward attainment of objectives. They bring consistency of approach in problem solving and responding to critical situations in an effective manner. They define 'the organization's way' of doing things which helps employees go about their tasks quickly and easily. They define ways which allow managers to exercise control by exception and leave routine tasks to their team members. Lastly, they are useful in communicating with vendors and partners while providing required legal protection.

Implementing a vendor cyber risk management policy is a best practice for organizations looking to secure their organizational data from risks that could emanate from their vendors.

The objective of such a policy should be to identify and classify these risks and then outline the controls the company wishes to implement to mitigate these risk. Unfortunately, many organizations overlook the need for a specific vendor cyber risk management policy which sets requisite standards of online security and behavior, and instead focus their attention on their own security posture and systems. A report on "Security Risks of Third-Party Vendor Relationships" published by RiskManagementMonitor.com includes an infographic estimating that 60% of data breaches involve a third party and that only 52% of companies have security standards in place regarding third-party vendors and contractors.[3] Given the current cyber threat landscape, it is imperative that organizations design specific policies that define their security posture and provide standards, guidance, and controls that they can hold their partners and vendors accountable to. Not doing so can expose organizations to a variety of cyber threats and risks. Here are reasons why you should consider implementing a vendor cyber risk policy.

Any business enterprise ought to be worried about third and fourth parties that are provided access to their corporate network and their sensitive data. If your ecosystem consists of vendors, subcontractors, and partners, you automatically offer more targets for cybercriminals to exploit. Organizations today increasingly rely on vendors and partners who bring specific expertise and specialized service offerings. However, we must remember that a larger number of vendors means more vulnerabilities and therefore risks. While third-party cyber risk is today an acknowledged risk to business, organizations are not doing enough to address it. In many ways, a well-articulated policy is an important first step.

The Importance of a Vendor Cyber Risk Policy

Most organizations today have become aware of cyber risks which are related to their own information systems, but the same level of identification and understanding of risks that are posed to them via their vendors' systems is limited due to low visibility of their information systems and security procedures. Apart from this, there is little or limited knowledge regarding the processes that vendors follow to vet their own personnel, what kind of access they have to the data, systems, or facilities of their customers, how they vet their service providers, and how they vet their IT products and software.

Organizations across sectors from finance to healthcare are today covered under the ambit of various laws and regulations related to cyber risks and data protection. Many of these regulations also specify how companies should manage their third-, fourth-, and nth-party risk. Policies and procedures implemented by these organizations must reflect and ensure compliance with the rules prescribed therein. Regulators are cognizant of the fact that data breaches through third and fourth parties can result in important and sometimes disastrous consequences and have shaped various regulations and guidelines to make sure that organizations pay due attention to the management of their supply chain and partner cyber risks. The absence of a vendor cyber risk management policy (especially in a regulated industry) can land you in trouble by making you not compliant. It is noteworthy that while you can outsource various activities to third parties, the legal risk and liabilities will remain with your organization.

The absence of a vendor cyber risk management policy can lead to a variety of cybercrimes, with outcomes ranging from data disruption to economic loss and loss of reputation. The 2013 Target breach is often cited as a failure to manage vendor-related risks. Cybercriminals got into Target's network after they hacked a third-party vendor who provided heating, ventilation, and air conditioning services. Data pertaining to more than 60M customers and 40M credit/debit cards was compromised. Target had to compensate up to $10,000 to each customer who had been impacted because of the breach. There were several reasons for the breach, but one that stands out today is that it emanated from the access rights granted to a third-party vendor that allowed hackers to gain access to Target's systems.

Another aspect of not having a proactive stance on vendor cyber risk management is that it will leave you exposed to vulnerabilities and risks that you are not even aware of. Not all vendor risks are easily identifiable and understandable. Outsourcing and partnerships are undertaken by many organizations without due process or diligence and even sharing with potential vendors as to what is expected of them. Policies are extremely useful in familiarizing employees and vendors (as well as their staff) with not only your security posture or intent, but also communicating the minimum operating standards that are expected of them.

For a long time, diligence has been limited to checklists and site visits, but today's cyber threat landscape demands much more circumspection on various aspects of cybersecurity. We are rapidly moving toward a 'trust and verify' model from a model where trust was based on self-declaration by vendors.

While the vulnerabilities of the supply chain are being increasingly targeted by cybercriminals, organizations have also come to realize that while they can outsource anything to vendors and third parties, the responsibility and liability for data loss rests with them.

Creating a Vendor Cyber Risk Management Policy

The creation of an officially documented vendor or third-party cyber risk management policy is the foundation for developing a vendor cyber risk management program and is vital for the success of the program. Such policies and procedures must address several types of cyber risks not only from data protection point of view but also business continuity and time to recover risks in the case of any cyber incident.

Policy creation is assumed to be a one-time activity, however, in a dynamically changing world, organizations will need to periodically revisit their policies and procedures, and make appropriate changes based on learnings and latest threat assessments.

According to Gartner,[4]

> VRM is the process of ensuring that the use of IT suppliers and service providers does not have a negative impact on business performance or create an unacceptable potential for business disruption. VRM ensures that enterprises analyze, monitor, and manage their risk exposure from the third-party vendors that offer services and IT products, or that have access to corporate's critical information.

Developing a vendor cyber risk policy and related procedures is a multi-stage process as given below:[5]

Stage 1. Preparation

Build a Vendor Cyber Risk Management team

It is critical to have people from many distinct positions and perspectives on your vendor cyber risk management team. Other than representation from top management, representation from procurement, legal, IT Security, and business units is required to gain a better understanding of data sharing with business associates. Once constituted, this team can start by gathering a list of vendors and all information related to vendors that their organization has collected.

Gathering Information

Compiling a list of all vendors/business associates that constitute your extended enterprise and what data and information systems they have access to will define the scope of the vendor cyber risk management exercise. Here, the definition of a vendor must be kept in mind to include every third party, supplier, consultant contractor, etc. – all associates your organization does business with or works in partnership with.

Classification & Prioritization of Vendors Based on Risk

At this stage it is important to understand using this list as to which vendors:

a. Are allowed to access your sensitive and important data
b. Are permitted direct access to your corporate network

This exercise will help in understanding which vendors are more important from a cyber risk point of view and help focus and direct attention toward them. If one of these vendors is compromised, it could lead to a harmful data breach.

This is not to say that other vendors must be out of the ambit of your security measures, but it enables you to prioritize. Any risk assessment should be based on the depth of your assessments based on the risk the vendors currently represent, as overtime vendors are likely to change.

Vendors can be classified based on the criticality of information that they have access to and the potential cyber risks that the organization can be put to in case their systems are compromised or penetrated by hackers. A fundamental step of VRM is the Vendor Risk Classification. A risk-based classification can enable you to construct a risk-based segmentation of your vendors.

Performing a vendor risk classification involves three (3) critical elements.[6] The first element is the creation of your vendor inventory as defined in the data gathering step above and identifying the data and systems that they have access to. The next element is classifying them based on a review of contracts with them, classifying risks of each vendor based on basic diligence like questionnaires, checklists, and meetings. The third element is to choose a method for risk assessment, such as off-site assessments, onsite assessments, and self-assessments or even a combination of all three methods.

Conducting a Risk Assessment

The risk assessment form and methodology that is used will have a profound bearing on the policy and procedure adopted. Identifying your critical and sensitive data and its access and exchange with participants of the extended enterprise is of prime importance. An objective assessment of threats and their potential adverse impact along with a detailed assessment of vendor/third-party systems, security measures, and data protection mechanisms form the core of the risk assessment. This is often achieved through diligence in the form of questionnaires, self-declaration by the vendors and interaction with their IT staff. This clearly is not enough in today's world where we are moving from 'trust' based policies and procedures to a 'trust-and-verify' based approach.

Determining how to conduct a risk assessment is one of the most difficult challenges for formulating a vendor cyber risk management program and related policies and procedures. Any methodology adopted must ensure that all risks are considered and prioritized, and suitable controls are put in place. Any omissions from a compliance or regulatory point of view could lead to unwanted regulatory intervention.

Assessments and diligence are conducted with clarity and speed and any procedures must recognize this. Stakeholders, while supporting thorough and comprehensive procedures, will expect speed of onboarding vendors. Teams framing policies and procedures can be hard pressed to strike a balance between caution and speed.

Standards, Regulations, and Specifying Minimum Requirements

There is always a pressing need to onboard new vendors and get on with integrating systems and operationalize partner relationships. However, there is no substitute for strong diligence and all-round clarity at this stage. Even as we understand the cybersecurity measures that our business partners have in place, they must be made aware of specific minimum requirements related to cyber risks along with guidelines, standards, and regulations that they would be held accountable for. While these are incorporated in Service Level Agreements (SLAs) that are part of present-day contracts, procedures must focus on the evidence that can demonstrate adherence to these. They must be strictly enforced, monitored, reviewed, and audited. Mechanisms for this must be a part of policy and procedure documentation.

Focus on Critical Risks with Higher Likelihood

Next, it is important to identify the types of cyber risks that you need to focus on. While all threats need to be addressed and the accompanying risks minimized, there will be certain areas like user authentication, user privileges, device security, role-based access to data, and other high-priority cybersecurity measures based on assessment of risks that must be prioritized.

Policy makers will be well advised to follow the principle of least privilege (POLP) within and across their extended enterprise. This entails the practice of limiting access rights for users to the bare minimum access permissions they need to perform their work. By implementing POLP, users can be allowed permission to read, write, or execute only those files or resources they require to do their work. Users are therefore granted the least amount of privilege necessary. POLP can also be applied to limiting access rights for applications, systems, processes, and devices to a bare minimum as is required to perform authorized activities.[7]

Another important principle that must be reflected in policies and procedures should be about layering your defenses. Perimeter security, though still relevant, is neither foolproof nor is it adequate. Building a layered defense enables organizations to become more resilient and enhance their chances of mitigating risks and must be embraced.

Stage 2. Drafting, Approving, and Communicating Policy

Policies and procedures are developed to meet the following:

a. In anticipation of need and
b. In response to need

It should not be considered a one-time activity as organizations need to constantly assess their business activities, objectives, responsibilities, and adapt to the threat environment.

The creation of an organizational vendor cyber risk policy must be owned and led by the top management of the organization. They may delegate the responsibility to an individual, working group, sub-committee, or staff members based on the expertise required. This person or group must consider not only requirements from a cyber threat viewpoint but also delve into the organization's regulatory legal responsibilities, commitment to standards, past experiences, and even seek external guidance and expertise in going about their task.

Drafting a policy is a task that requires a degree of foresight, learning from the past, and a clear articulation of requirements. Persons responsible for this must make sure that they are able to communicate the policy to those who will be expected to implement it. A vendor cyber risk policy must include, but not be limited to, the following:

a. Statement of policy and purpose
b. Scope and applicability
c. Periodicity of conducting risk assessments across the extended enterprise
d. Allocation of roles and responsibilities, physical and IT access controls
e. Responsibility for maintaining and updating the policy and procedures
f. Confidentiality and privacy agreements
g. Distribution and communication of policies and procedures
h. Information security obligations and controls
i. Configuration management, patching, and verification of system security controls
j. Standards and guidelines for vendors
k. Hiring and training of employees
l. SLAs
m. Minimum compliance and regulatory requirements
n. Required vendor controls – access controls, malware protection, data protection, etc.
o. Working toward adopting a zero-trust architecture across the extended enterprise
p. Cyber incident response co-operation
q. Testing security systems, certification, and auditing requirements
r. Costs and liabilities in the event of a data breach
s. Insurance requirements
t. Termination and contract closure – return or destruction of all information assets by the outsourcer after the completion of the outsourced activity
u. Monitoring and review
v. Disaster recovery, business continuity requirements
w. Verification of security controls through contract and documentation

Stakeholder consultation is an especially important part of framing policies. For policies to be effective, those affected should be consulted and their support enlisted by offering the opportunity to consider and discuss the potential implications of the policy. Stakeholders could include departmental/functional heads, management committee members, and users.

Policies must be approved at the highest levels of an organization. An empowered management committee which is responsible for all policies and procedures in the organization must approve the policy before it is implemented. This will ensure better acceptance all around and enable better enforcement. The management committee is accountable for all policies and their proper implementation within the organization.

To support policies, it is also important to determine the processes and procedures that are required to support them. Clear operating guidelines need to be laid out detailing what is to be done, who is going to do it, what actions are to be taken in the case of an exception, etc. For this, the engagement of a larger group of people may be required to consider different situations and scenarios. The focus here should not be just related to preventing cyber threats and minimizing risks, but also procedures to be followed in the event of a cyber incident.

Determining the level of access that needs to be provided to a given vendor is a crucial element, as not all vendors need the same level of access to sensitive data, network, and information technology systems to do their work.

It is also a good practice, before a policy is approved, to solicit a last round of feedback from stakeholders to address any residual concerns, make any final changes, and even gain their support before implementation.

Stage 3. Implementation

Implementing policies and procedures involves translating the objectives and guidelines into the organization's functioning and operations. The process of communicating and empowering those who will be actively implementing policies is a particularly crucial step for the success of a vendor cyber risk management program. Roles and responsibilities should be made clear so that operating personnel can proceed with their activities and tasks with speed and clarity.

Policies and procedures must incorporate aspects like a vendor's failure to provide and maintain agreed service and security levels, compliance failures, etc. and detail alternate plans and actions.

Establishing a transparent relationship that fosters co-operation with vendors is essential for the success of a vendor cyber risk management program. Policies and procedures fail when vendors will not provide information, reports, access, and evidence of security controls and compliance.

'Trust but verify' is an important concept that is strongly gaining ground in cybersecurity and is even being made mandatory by regulatory agencies. Organizations can and must trust vendors and business associates who work with them but is increasingly becoming necessary to verify that their cybersecurity procedures meet their standards and in regulated industries, and compliance requirements.

Conducting Due Diligence

The practice of doing due diligence before onboarding vendors has existed for a long time. However, the importance and depth of due diligence from a cyber risk perspective has never been as critical as it is today. Procedures for conducting due diligence must be clearly spelled out and strictly enforced. Cybersecurity due diligence must be aimed at identifying and remediating the cyber risks of third-party vendors. This involves collecting information that provides insights into a third-party vendor's existing cybersecurity posture and IT security efforts. Tools often used by organizations are checklists, questionnaires, site visits, and interaction between IT and IT security teams. To minimize cyber risks in the active threat landscape of today, organizations seek certifications, compliance to standards and conduct third-party audits to gain greater visibility into vendor systems and practices to bolster cybersecurity efforts across the extended expertise.

Stage 4. Monitoring, Reviewing, and Revising

Vendor cyber risk management is a continuous process. It calls for constant vigilance and monitoring to determine what is happening on not just the enterprise network, but that of the extended enterprise. This is required to ensure that your vendors ensure they are meeting your cybersecurity standards and expectations. Constant vigilance can lower the probability of your organization becoming a victim of a cyber-attack or data breach via your supply chain.

From a monitoring and reporting perspective, policies and procedures including important security controls, such as access usage, vulnerability scanning and penetration testing reports, compliance areas, etc., must be examined and assessed.

While monitoring involves gathering and analyzing many parameters and metrics, experience tells us that the key areas to look out for are privileged credential theft (remember Target?). Hackers often use this technique to gain access to organization systems via their vendor systems and then move laterally to cause maximum damage and disruption.

Effective monitoring of vendor cyber risk requires a degree of transparency, collaboration, and trust between the partnering entities. While specific metrics can be derived based on an organization's risk assessment and threat perception, some of the key areas are:

- Threat intelligence and monitoring
- Access control and user privileges and configuration management
- Cyber hygiene and security posture
- Adherence/compliance with standards and regulations
- Status of security certifications and ratings if any
- Performance aspects as per SLAs

Reviews must be conducted periodically with all business associates regarding contractual obligations outlined in the risk management policy and in SLAs. The auditing process can be a particularly useful mechanism for conducting reviews related to the effectiveness of policies and procedures. Audits can help review the effectiveness of policies, third-party risk assessment mechanisms, and controls. They can provide insights into due diligence, risk monitoring, compliance, contract management, and other key areas. Audits can be helpful in formulating new policies based on assessment of the bigger cybersecurity picture and objectives and ensure that procedures are well aligned with objectives.

While organizations take care and exercise due diligence while onboarding partners, full due diligence is required (sometimes defined by regulators) at a frequency that must be clearly defined in the cyber risk management policy. Typically, all critical and high-risk vendors must undergo a full due diligence review annually.

When contracts come up for renewal, there is another opportunity to include new requirements to keep systems and data secure, according to the latest best practices and industry standards. Such reviews may help in reviewing earlier policies and procedures and conducting fresh audits.

Cyber risks are not static. On the contrary, the cyber threat and technology landscape is always changing. Hence, it is imperative that policy and procedures are revised from time to time or to address critical issues that were not anticipated earlier. Policy framers must define procedures and ownership for revisions and updates to policies and maintain it as a 'living' document.

Policies, Procedures, Standards, and Best Practices

For drawing up effective and time-tested policies and procedures for vendor cyber risk management, policy makers can reference standards like National Institute of Standards and Technology (NIST), International Standards Organization (ISO), maturity models such as Cybersecurity Maturity Model Certification (CMMC), and regulations such as the California Consumer Privacy Protection Act (CCPA), the Health Insurance Portability and Accountability Act (HIPAA), and other such sources which provide guidance on vendor cyber risk management and assimilate best practices and help in enhancing cybersecurity standards.

Summary

Policies and procedures are necessary to ensure consistency in an organizations operation. They must provide clarity and guidance in dealing with matters and activities that are central to the organization's functioning such as health and safety, risk management, regulatory requirements, or issues that may have more severe consequences.

Benefits of well-defined policies and procedures are many. Policies and procedures empower employees and managers to clearly understand individual, team responsibilities, save time, and direct resources toward attainment of objectives. They bring consistency of approach in problem solving and responding to critical situations in an effective manner. They define 'the organization's way' of doing things which helps employees go about their tasks quickly and easily.

Policies that are clearly defined, written, effectively communicated to, and understood by all stakeholders can fulfill the purpose for which they are made. In the context of vendor cyber risk management, policies and procedures will often be put to the test and therefore they need to consider different risk scenarios and adapt in response to emerging situations and threats.

Notes

1   Definition of Vendor Risk Management (VRM) (n.d.). Gartner information technology glossary. Retrieved August 31, 2020, from https://www.gartner.com/en/information-technology/glossary/vendor-risk-management.
2   www.diycommitteeguide.org (n.d.). Policy development for management committees. https://dictionary.cambridge.org/dictionary/english/procedure.
3   Policy (2024). https://dictionary.cambridge.org/dictionary/essential-british-english/policy.
4   Procedure (2024). https://dictionary.cambridge.org/dictionary/english/procedure.
5   McDonald, C. (2018, September 20). Security risks of third-party vendor relationships|Risk Management Monitor. https://www.riskmanagementmonitor.com/security-risks-of-third-party-vendor-relationships/.
6   Third-Party security: vendor classification, assessment & management. (n.d.). Systèmes De Sécurité Hitachi. https://www.hitachi-systems-security.com/blog/third-party-security-vendor-classification-assessment-management.
7   Gillis, A. S. (2023, September 26). Principle of least privilege (POLP). Security. https://searchsecurity.techtarget.com/definition/principle-of-least-privilege-POLP.

19

INTERNAL AUDIT

Role of Internal Audit in the Three Lines of Defense

For many vendor risk practitioners, the thought of being examined by an Internal Audit team compares to a root canal. It is often an unpleasant corporate reality and a frustrating afterthought, resulting in an adversarial relationship. It is understandable why many would not be comfortable with an internal group unpicking their work and pointing out deficiencies to the senior management team. It does not have to be that way, and in fact we will teach you how to change your mindset to embrace Internal Audit to enable you to develop a better vendor risk program.

First, let us clarify where Internal Audit fits into the overall risk management structure. Three Lines of Defense is a popular model found in multiple risk management frameworks such as COSO[1] or ISO 31000.[2]

The First Line of Defense: is operationally handled by front-line managers who have day-to-day responsibility over risks and controls. The first line designs and operates controls to maximize the likelihood that corporate objectives

DOI: 10.4324/9781003581321-22

are achieved and risks stay within stated risk tolerances. Everyone is a risk manager and responsible for managing risks within their specific roles.

Second Line of Defense: is handled by oversight, internal monitoring, and credible challenge function that owns the enterprise risk management framework. It supports the executive management team with risk management expertise and monitoring hand-in-hand with the first line to ensure that risks and controls are properly managed. Based on industry and company size, second line may also actually develop or modify internal control and risk management processes, in addition to providing a credible challenge. Vendor risk management programs may sit within either Line 1, Line 2, or a hybrid.

Third Line of Defense (Internal Audit): assures executive management and the board that Line 1 and Line 2 are meeting expectations of their commitments. Line 3 uses a systematic approach to audit the effectiveness of risk management, internal control, and governance processes. It is critical that Internal Audit is independent and objective.

Given the Internal Audit role as the Third Line of Defense, you can expect a periodic audit of the vendor risk program and related processes. Internal Audit will work with the management team to determine the right timing of the audit and will typically publish their audit plan.

For regulated entities, regulators may also conduct an examination of vendor risk programs. Any internal documents are discoverable by regulators and should be shared upon request. For larger enterprises there are typically internal groups that specialize in managing communications with the regulators and can assist in facilitating regulatory exams. Regulators will have access to the results of Internal Audits, and one of the success criteria of the Internal Audit team is to find and remediate issues before regulators do.

Expected Evidence

So, what can you expect during an Internal Audit? Typically, an audit plan defines a list of control objectives, associated controls, and required evidence to demonstrate each control is in place. You may be asked for detailed documentation and walkthroughs to demonstrate your policies and controls are operating effectively. Based on the criticality of a control, you may be asked for a sample or a full listing of artifacts. The Internal Audit team is likely to review your vendor inventory, your assessment process and pick a small number of vendors for a deep dive into how they are being managed and assessed for risk.

Key Differences of Internal Audit vs Vendor Audit

Internal Audit is different from a third-party vendor audit by your customers. In Chapter 20, we will detail what you can expect in a vendor audit and best practices on how you should strategically deal with it. The Internal Audit is often much more thorough and deeper. During an Internal Audit, you need to share any requested information, unlike in a vendor audit where you can offer screen shares, interviews, or redacted summary documents.

Key differences:

- Full access to all evidence vs an arm-length engagement (there are no confidentiality clauses to hide behind in an Internal Audit).
- Internal Audit is conducted over an extended period of time (typically months), vs days or at most weeks in a vendor audit.
- Internal Audit includes testing for effectiveness of controls and sample testing vs vendor audit is typically limited to design of controls with no or limited effectiveness testing.
- Resulting Internal Audit findings are reported and tracked by the management team vs vendor audit tracked by the customer.
- Internal Audit team may partner with you and advise you throughout your development and execution of the vendor risk program, whereas a vendor audit is a point-in-time activity.

The Mindset of Being Ready

The best way to deal with an Internal Audit is not to fear it, but to embrace it. The Internal Audit team is not there to embarrass you or tell you that you are doing a bad job, but it's there to protect the enterprise and ensure regulatory examination readiness. You should never have a mindset of doing something because of regulators or Internal Audit but instead to have the right controls and manage risk for the company.

We Recommend Ten Best Practices

1. Publish vendor risk management policy and standards – ensure that you either have a standalone policy or embed vendor risk in relevant company policies and/or standards.

2. Map business processes – ensure that your critical business processes are mapped and well-documented for the entire cybersecurity vendor risk life cycle.

3. Maintain operating procedures – update your operating procedures in support of your policy and business processes and ensure that they are periodically reviewed and signed off by appropriate stakeholders and management.

4. Document your key controls – within each business process, document key controls and ensure that the operating procedures support each control in detail.

5. Develop a training and communications plan – identify training needs for your new and existing staff, with periodic refreshes of the curriculum. An effective training program ensures that your operating procedures are clear, well-understood, and staff actually follows it.

6. Identify and report self-identified gaps – proactively seek out and document gaps. Encourage your team to find and report issues before the Internal Audit does and openly share these issues with Internal Audit.

7. Track remediation plans for self-identified issues – formally track commitment dates and milestones for each issue and ensure accountability for getting remediation completed.

8. Automate key controls whenever possible – proactively prioritize automation opportunities and leverage reporting and analytics for managing your key controls. While it is not practical to have most controls fully automated, use technology to enhance the quality of key controls.

9. Conduct Quality Assurance – establish a role or a team that proactively focuses on testing your processes and key controls. Quality Assurance is typically a First Line of Defense activity and picks up issues prior to Internal Audit. Quality Assurance is typically a major source of self-identified control gaps.

10. Establish a roadmap for maturing your controls – tell a story to your management and key stakeholders about how you will reduce control gaps in your business processes over time. Vendor risk, just like

cybersecurity, is a journey without a destination. Control gaps will never be fully eliminated, and new gaps will continue to emerge all the time.

Engage with Internal Audit Throughout the Life Cycle

A common missed opportunity is to engage Internal Audit only during an actual audit. That is a misconception, and actually the Internal Audit team is frequently more than happy to engage throughout the life cycle of your program. Regular engagement is a win-win for both you and the Internal Audit team, as that streamlines the Audit process and gives you the benefit of their advice and guidance. Here are some suggestions:

- Include Internal Audit on your Steering Committees and Forums.
- Consult with Internal Audit proactively when making key design decisions.
- Discuss and provide input for the Internal Audit plan. You may be able to influence timing and scope.
- Have regular checkpoints with Internal Audit key contacts to stay coordinated with their plans for automation, key concerns, or industry trends.
- Establish professional relationships with Internal Audit leaders.

They are often a great source of insights and offer valuable perspectives. We often find that Internal Audit professionals take leadership roles in leading Technology Risk, Cybersecurity, or Vendor Risk functions. Their experience in Internal Audit makes them solid candidates for developing and managing controls. Internal Audit staff can be a valuable recruitment pipeline and in some cases can be your next boss or a peer.

Dealing with Internal Audit Findings

No matter how ready you are, what best practices you follow, and how you condition yourself to have a positive mindset, chances are you will have to deal with Internal Audit findings. Your goal should be to get a satisfactory report, possibly with low- or medium-severity observations.

Throughout the process, the Internal Audit team will typically share with you their concerns and draft observations, giving you an opportunity to alleviate their concerns before these concerns end up as issues in the report. Internal Audit team does not always have experience in your specific domain, company, or industry. The auditor may mark something as an issue, where in fact you may feel strongly otherwise. In these cases, you should absolutely have a discussion and attempt to explain and demonstrate evidence and/or compensating controls.

Here Are the Top Don'ts

- Never get emotional or take disagreements personally.
- Never try to influence the auditor in a way that is considered unethical or illegal (do not even think about bribes or personal favors).
- Never insult or threaten the auditor (yes, we have seen it happen).
- Never fabricate evidence for controls that are not in place (that is unethical, likely illegal, and not aligned with your company's policy).

Here Are the Top Do's

- Ask for a draft report.
- Argue in a professional way for addressing draft findings where you believe there is a compensating control.
- Point the auditor toward your self-identified control gaps (it is perfectly fine if the final report references these gaps, as long as it is indicated as self-identified).
- Respect auditor's final determination.

Once the report is final, you can expect that the findings will be formally tracked followed by a remediation plan. If you are new to the function, the audit report will be informative to help you shape the roadmap. In that case an unsatisfactory audit can be a catalyst for change and can even help you get funding.

In case you get an unsatisfactory audit for a function where you are a long-standing incumbent, you should be ready for a conversation with your management on how it got to that point and what you will do differently. That is unfortunately not a career enhancer, and we have seen many cases where careers were ruined and year-end compensation suffered.

A satisfactory audit report should be celebrated and provide reassurance about the quality of your program.

Notes

1 "Committee of Sponsoring Organizations of the Treadway Commission Enterprise Risk Management Integrating with Strategy and Performance", Coso.org, June 2017, https://www.coso.org/enterprise-risk-management.
2 "Risk Management ISO31000", ISO.org, February 2018, https://www.iso.org/files/live/sites/isoorg/files/store/en/PUB100426.pdf.

20

THIRD-PARTY VENDOR AUDIT

The Snowball Effect

In prior chapters we introduced a concept of snowball effect resulting from increased regulatory push for transparency. The volume of customer questionnaires and audit requests continues to grow as continued regulatory and cybersecurity pressures demand customers to extend their risk assessments to their supply chain. We discussed the three types of vendor due diligence and how to get it right. Here is the twist, every customer is also a vendor to someone else. For example, global banks are notorious for being tough on their vendors in due diligence requests. At the same time, banks as vendors often do not reciprocate the levels of transparency they demand from their own supply chain, even if it comes from their peer banks.

There are generally three types of customer requests: onsite assessments (vendor audits), desktop (remote assessments), and self-attestation/questionnaires. It is the reciprocal part of what we discussed in Chapter 16 when we covered how customers assess their vendors.

DOI: 10.4324/9781003581321-23

Onsite Assessments (Vendor Audit)

If you are providing critical services to a regulated industry or processing confidential data, then brace yourself for onsite assessment requests. It may come in many shapes and names, like vendor audit, onsite due diligence, or comprehensive assessment. At times, you might not immediately recognize that the request includes an onsite assessment, as it might initially appear as a simple vendor questionnaire.

You can expect that your customers will want to peek into your control environment, policies, and procedures. Some assessments will just be a check-the-box exercise, and some on a mission to find some deficiencies. Common characteristics of onsite assessments include:

- A one-day or multi-day visit to one or more physical locations.
- Preparatory work, acquiring initial responses from you through a questionnaire and pinpointing specific focus areas.
- Getting access to internal documents or a series of interviews, screen shares, and process walkthroughs that are otherwise considered too sensitive to share outside of physical walls.
- Going beyond control design assessment and testing control effectiveness for certain controls by looking at small samples. Sample of one is common, unlike a Systems and Organizational Controls (SOC) report that looks for a much larger sample over a period of time.
- Performing physical security review, by looking at data centers, physical access controls, and potentially health and safety.

The COVID-19 pandemic brought an interesting dimension to onsite assessments. To cope with closed offices and prohibited travel there has been increased willingness by CISOs to screen share more sensitive information that previously was only available onsite. Additionally, some remote assessments turned into deeper reviews and creative approaches emerged such as specialized screen sharing tools that prevent screen capture or CCTV footage of data centers that can serve as evidence of physical security.

Desktop (a.k.a. Remote Assessments)

Desktop assessments are a cornerstone of vendor risk assessment programs. Like onsite assessments, depth and quality can vary. In many cases desktop assessments can be more robust than onsite assessments.

Common Characteristics of Desktop Assessments Include:

- A one-day or multi-day series of screen sharing sessions or phone interviews, preceded by preparation work, of getting preliminary responses from a vendor to a questionnaire and identifying specific areas of focus.
- Getting access to internal documents or a series of interviews, screen shares, and process walkthroughs that were deemed to be not too sensitive to share outside of physical walls.
- Typically limited to control design assessment and not actually testing control effectiveness by looking at small samples. In cases of control effectiveness, a sample of one is most common, unlike a SOC report that looks for a much larger sample over a period of time.
- Typically excluding actual physical security reviews but may review policies and procedures for physical reviews.

Self-Attestations and Questionnaires

Some may consider self-attestations as a form of vendor due diligence. For example, a question of "Do you have an Information Security Policy Y/N?" is considered a self-attestation. Alternatively, "Do you have an Information Security Policy Y/N? and please attach if applicable" is not a self-attestation.

Typically, some self-attestation questions can be included as part of a desktop assessment and may guide more targeted follow-ups if appropriate. An assessment that is mostly based on self-attestations offers limited value and can be used for lower risk vendors. The volume of these questionnaires can be significant and continues to grow. Some questionnaires can be overbearing, either asking for seemingly unreasonable information or having an excessive number of questions.

Why It Is Strategically Important to Get It Right

There are five primary reasons for responding efficiently and correctly to customer due diligence requests:

1. Operational efficiency of keeping up with request volume
2. Revenue from new customers, commercial renewals, or additional products/services

3. Liability for providing incorrect information in case of being sued by customers after a data breach
4. Customer perception of being secure, transparent, and easy to do business with
5. Enterprise security of not divulging overly confidential information that may expose the company to attack vectors

Operational efficiency: the immediate objective is to keep up with the volume and intensity of requests. It is important to define processes, operating procedures, and Service Level Agreements for each request type. It is about having an operational mindset of establishing and running customers' requests as a business process.

Revenue implications: a frequent blind spot is treating customer due diligence requests as a necessary back-office evil and being disconnected from revenue-generating activities. The fact is that these requests often influence new customers' business, commercial renewals, additional purchases, or at times revenue protection from struggling relationships. It is critical to be responsive and aligned with the business development team and drive a customer-driven mindset, no matter how frustrating these requests may be.

Liability for providing inaccurate information: providing inaccurate information as part of the questionnaires is not only a customer reputation issue but can become a legal liability in case of a data breach. Imagine if your company is part of a lawsuit after a material data breach, and information you provided to your customers can be construed as misleading or untruthful.

Customer perception: it is a small world, and there is a well-known list of companies that have a reputation for being difficult to deal with as part of the due diligence process. On the other hand, there are vendors that go out of their way to be transparent and efficient to offer a reasonable level of security assurance to their customers. Brand equity matters and projects confidence to customers and partners.

Enterprise security: the other extreme of not co-operating with customers on requests for information is to freely share confidential internal documents, vulnerabilities, and control weaknesses with all your customers. Many CISOs developed specific guiding principles or policies regarding what can be shared with customers. For example, it is okay to share redacted internal policies or potentially do screen sharing of fragments of internal policies. Sharing a summary of penetration or business continuity test results

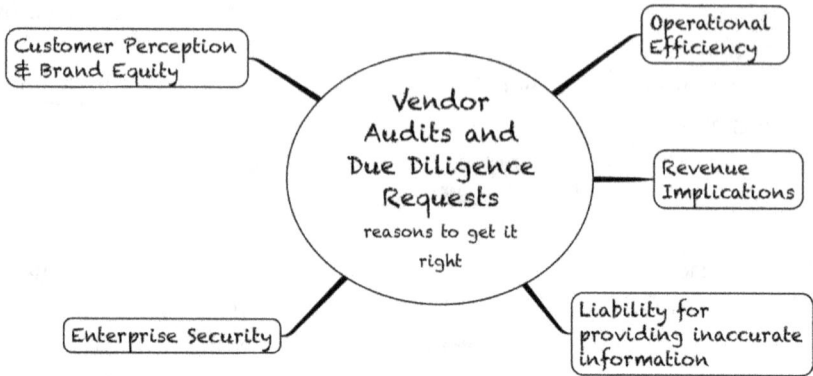

Figure 20.1 Reasons to Get It Right

is usually acceptable. Sharing the actual details of such documents can add unnecessary risk of exploitation of known vulnerabilities in your risk posture (Figure 20.1).

Options to Structure Internally to React to Customer Requests

Many medium and large enterprises have dedicated teams on both sides of chasing vendors and answering requests as a vendor. As a best practice there are typically two models that work well:

- A dedicated centralized team that services all requests
- Embedded responsibility for account management team, supported by various support groups, consistent tooling, and document repositories

In smaller companies, there is typically a designated person most familiar with handling customers' due diligence requests. That person may be a CISO or his/her delegate.

Decision on which model to use is often driven by consistency in how product offerings fit into a unified control environment. For example, if every product and service is customized for each customer and has different controls, then the second option may be more appropriate. Alternatively, if all products are supported by the same set of controls, then a centralized team approach works well.

Some diagnostic questions may include:

- Is your account management team aware of the process for routing customers' audit requests or questionnaires?
- Is there a robust set of internal resources to help the team to consistently answer questionnaires or respond to audit requests?
- Is there an escalation process for your account management team for handling customer complaints associated with due diligence requests?

If the answer is "No" to any of these questions, then more work is required to get it right.

Commercial "Bullying"

You should feel empowered to push back on customer requests that are not reasonable, but you may face commercial pressures to still respond. That commercial pressure may come as an escalation from senior business leaders who are trying to close a hot deal or maintain a customer relationship. However, revenue often trumps everything, and business executives may not fully appreciate what you consider unreasonable.

It is important to provide clarity to the business team on key considerations and have a formal process to escalate your concerns. The likelihood of pressures is higher for new customers than periodic due diligence requests, as an overzealous business development executive may try harder to meet his/her sales target.

Large customers, especially banks, are notorious for demanding deep audits from their vendors. Smaller companies and FinTechs may not have enough resources or technical ability to satisfy such requests. Therefore, being prepared to handle these commercial pressures is critical for business success.

Shift from Reactive to Proactive

To tackle the snowball effect, here are the top ten best practices to consider.

1. *Maximize usage of usage certifications that are most relevant to your customers:* refer to prior chapters on discussion regarding common independent

attestation reports (such as SOC 2), certifications, domain-specific standards, common questionnaire standards, and working with shared assessment utilities or approaches. Prioritize your adoption based on expected demand from your customers.

2. *Create a library of redacted policies, procedures, and common evidence to be available on internal portal for those who are involved in customer due diligence requests:* consider establishing governance and procedures of who and how one can share this information.

3. *Establish robust tooling to answer questions:* consider creating a customer-facing portal that can share your vendor certification information, frequently asked questions, and questionnaires on a self-service basis. Google Cloud is a good example of a self-service customer-facing portal.[1] In some cases, vendors make a robust evidence inventory available to their customers, where access is only physically allowed onsite, forcing customers to take time and expense. There are multiple solutions that help with automation of customer due diligence responses. Some solutions include RiskQ, OneTrust, and S&P Global KY3P.

4. *Standardize internal processes for answering questions and responding to vendor audits:* including an operating model of how much of the process is centralized vs decentralized based on considerations outlined in the earlier section of this chapter.

5. *Exercise caution in managing audit rights:* refer to Chapter 15 for details on terms to incorporate into legal contracts, RFx, specifically addressing the right to audit. You should establish an internal control with your contracting team to seek special approvals before such rights are granted and request that customers pay a fee for an audit right or leverage an industry assessment utility that you work with to conduct such audits. At a minimum, the audit right should be limited in frequency to avoid excessive requests.

6. *Check if the customer is truly your customer:* it may sound obvious, but under normal circumstances you should only honor vendor audit and questionnaire requests from your actual contractual customers.

7. *Control third-party access:* when a customer utilizes a third party to conduct an assessment on their behalf, evaluate Non-Disclosure Agreement (NDA) and confidentiality provisions before proceeding.

8. *Be clear on scope and services:* even if your customer is truly your customer, your team still needs to confirm what services your customer consumes and if their request corresponds to these services.

9. *Answer questions ahead of time:* for vendor audits answer any questionnaires and agree on agenda ahead of time to ensure availability of key personnel and a ring-fenced process.

10. *Review draft findings:* ensure that you have an opportunity to review draft findings before the customer finalizes their report for internal distribution. That enables you to clear out any miscommunications and avoid unnecessary issues.

Note

1   "Compliance offerings", *Google Cloud*, https://cloud.google.com/security/compliance/offerings.

PART IV

FUTURE PERSPECTIVES IN VENDOR CYBER RISK MANAGEMENT

21

THE WAY FORWARD

The Way Forward

When we deliberate on the way forward[1] for organizations in managing supply chain cyber risks,[2] we need to consider the following[3]:

1. The current supply chain cyber risk environment
2. Upcoming threats from emerging technologies
3. The impact of new regulations, standards, and frameworks
4. Developing and adopting an approach to safeguard supply chains against cyber risks

Before we consider each of the above, we need to examine the key challenges in managing supply chain cyber risks that many organizations are still grappling with:

1. Ensuring that cyber risk management within the organizations is well integrated across different levels of the organization. Absence of

DOI: 10.4324/9781003581321-25

collaboration across functions such as procurement, legal, IT, and other relevant departments pose a big challenge when it comes to addressing supply chain risks effectively.

2. Mapping out the supply chain, including sub-tier suppliers, to identify vulnerabilities and assess risks both at hardware and software levels is essential for risk assessment. Understanding the organization's entire supply chain is essential. Many organizations lack full visibility into their extended supply networks.

3. Identifying and managing critical components which are most important for an organization's operations and ensuring focus of security mechanisms on the high-impact components is a complex task. Maintaining software inventories (SBOMs) and identifying and addressing vulnerabilities across the supply chain is never easy.

4. Establishing close collaboration on cybersecurity with key suppliers is essential. Yet very often, organizations fail to classify their supplier based on their relative importance to meeting the organization's objectives, with whom sensitive data is shared and privileged access to information is granted to ensure efficiency and speed of operation. The task of conducting ongoing risk assessments and implementing joint mitigation efforts can be critical in warding off supply chain attacks that can cause great disruption and impact. Further, regular communication helps address emerging threats and adapt to changing circumstances.[4]

5. Another key challenge is the task of continuously assessing and monitoring suppliers throughout the relationship is critical. Here again, many organizations struggle to conduct regular risk assessments, audits, and performance evaluations to help maintain security and resilience.

Hence, organizations continue to struggle in managing supply chain cyber risks.

The Current Supply Chain Cyber Risk Environment

Cybercriminals today fully recognize the fact that while organizations can devote resources and investments to build robust cybersecurity and resilience at the organizational level, when it comes to implementing security measures across the supply chain it is a different ball game. Hence, supply chain attacks have become a favored tactic for cybercriminals. While senior executives across organizations often are aware that supply chain attacks offer cybercriminals a way to exploit interconnected systems, gain access to valuable resources, and evade detection, they fail to take appropriate action to protect against it. Supply chain cyber risk is still an underestimated risk and needs to be prioritized in order to proactively manage supply chain risks, safeguard their networks and data, as well as prepare to meet the forthcoming challenges.

A closer look at some of the significant supply chain cyber-attacks that took place in 2023 will help us gain an understanding of the current methods and actions deployed by cybercriminals.

After the SolarWinds cyber incident that impacted even government agencies and Fortune 500 firms, cybercriminals have recognized the fact that a compromised software component can flow unimpeded through a supply chain, affecting downstream systems.

CLOP, a Russian-speaking cybercriminal organization known for its multilevel extortion techniques (it has extorted more than $500 million in ransom payments, targeting major organizations worldwide) made headlines by exploiting MOVEit (a commonly used file transfer utility) vulnerability in supply chains to launch attacks on high-profile targets like the New York City Department of Education, UCLA, Siemens Energy, and Big Four accounting firms. The MOVEit breach is among the most devastating exploitation of a zero-day vulnerability ever. The sheer magnitude of the attack is such that it is estimated to have impacted 122 organizations and exposed the data of roughly 15 million people. Cybercriminals continue to identify vulnerabilities that can cause widespread damage by exploiting any attack vector that allows them to compromise systems and demand ransoms.[5] Microsoft too attributed attacks on PaperCut servers (a software application designed to help organizations manage printing) to the CLOP and LockBit (another cybercriminal group ransomware operations, which exploited vulnerabilities to steal corporate data.[6]

Other tactics employed by cybercriminals include the exploitation of third-party relationships and trusted connections to infiltrate organizations. In April 2023, a North Korean hacking group conducted a major supply chain attack against a Voice over Internet Protocol (VoIP) communication company.

Phishing continues to be the foremost initial access vector. Threat actors have become adept at exploiting human vulnerabilities and lack of security awareness to bait users to reveal sensitive information or granting unauthorized access.[7] Instances of email compromise continue to remain a common initial access point to infiltrate supply chains are on the rise. Cybercriminals are targeting organizations increasingly using deepfakes to enhance phishing and social engineering campaigns. These campaigns target individuals within organizations and supply chain participants, tricking them into performing actions that compromise security. The use of deepfake videos or audio messages boosts the chances of deceiving employees into revealing confidential credentials or transferring funds to accounts controlled by cybercriminals.

A new attack vector in the form of physical goods has emerged which could infiltrate computing supply chains causing devastating consequences. An example of this is the Supermicro case. Here, Chinese agents are alleged to have inserted a chip into motherboards used by computers deployed by banks and the US Department of Defense.[8] This attack vector has the potential to infiltrate computing supply chains which can lead to devastating consequences.

The supply chain cyber risk environment today is a supercharged one with hackers using various types of threats including ransomware, data breaches, password sniffing/cracking software, spoofing attacks, and direct hacking. These threats pose significant risks as they can impact suppliers, even disrupt the entire supply chain, and ultimately impact customer demands.

Upcoming Threats from Emerging Technologies

Emerging technologies are constantly shaping our world. The pace of technological change has accelerated significantly over the years having a transformative impact on our world, but at the same time creating new security concerns. Let us examine the top five technologies that will have major security implications for supply chain risk management.

Artificial Intelligence

Artificial intelligence (AI) covers a spectrum of technologies including learning, natural language processing, and neural networks. A new form of AI known as Generative Artificial Intelligence holds promise in enhancing supply chain resilience. While traditional AI is useful for analyzing data using algorithms and data to make autonomous decisions, learn from previous experiences, and adapt to new situations and perform specific tasks, Generative AI focuses on creating new content like text, images, and music.[9] It also enables computers to execute tasks that typically require human intelligence.

Generative AI has rapidly emerged as a fundamental technology for a variety of applications. It empowers substantial progress in manufacturing and various enterprise applications by creating synthetic content, data, and images. Additionally, it optimizes operational models, designs, and process simulations, while extracting valuable insights from operational data.

As is the case, with the introduction of new technologies, there are new security concerns that need to be addressed. Generative AI models require the use of Large Language Models (LLMs) to create and generate human-like text based on the data it has been trained on. The LLMs play an important role in advancing Generative AI, especially in natural language processing. These LLMs are essential for understanding and interpreting human language, enabling them to produce contextually appropriate responses. LLMs have the ability to comprehend the meaning and nuances within sentences, making them a key requirement for applications like chatbots, content creation, and machine translation. They also enable search engines and virtual assistants in answering questions and providing precise and insightful responses.

Generative AI applications usually provide a human-like interface. This feature can be exploited by cybercriminals using tools such as WormGPT to launch phishing or business email compromise attacks.[10] Supply chain professionals should be wary of AI-generated content and verify the authenticity of communications before interacting with them.

Training of Generative AI models requires large volumes of data which includes sensitive information related to suppliers, customers, and internal processes. Ensuring data security and privacy of this data is crucial to prevent unauthorized access or data breaches. Creation of Generative AI models using contaminated or synthetic data sets can lead to introduction of biases in decision-making or infringement of privacy rights. Furthermore, Generative AI tools operate autonomously, with little or no human intervention leading to challenges in auditing and monitoring. Generative AI has high dependence on input data quality. Often, the quality of data from supply chain partners may not be reliable and could lead to unexpected results.

Deepfake technology, a form of Generative AI has taken the world by storm and is rapidly becoming a major cybersecurity threat. Cybercriminals are leveraging AI and machine learning to create synthetic or manipulated digital content, including images, videos, audio, and text. Since these deepfakes are remarkably like their real counterparts, by replicating or altering appearance, voice, mannerisms, or language, they have the ability to deceive humans and even autonomous systems into trusting that the content is authentic. Using deepfakes, threat actors can launch highly sophisticated social engineering campaigns that could help them infiltrate and penetrate supply chains.[11] For example, deepfake videos or audio messages could more often than not deceive employees into disclosing confidential information credentials or transferring funds to accounts controlled by the threat actors.[12] Deepfakes pose an alarming threat to society as they are capable of spreading misinformation and manipulating information and creating false narratives that can cause great harm to organizations and society. Considering the serious damage which deepfakes can cause, the World Economic Forum has recognized this as a major potential threat to businesses.

Organizations must stay vigilant and take proactive steps to defend against deepfake-enhanced cyber-attacks and scams. Educating employees about the risks of deepfakes, implementing robust authentication mechanisms, and monitoring for suspicious activity are essential strategies to mitigate this emerging threat.

Generative AI is increasingly being leveraged by threat actors to create advanced forms of malware that can bypass traditional security systems. These include polymorphic and adaptive malware strains which can dynamically change their code, making it difficult for signature-based detection systems to identify and prevent them. Another way in which Generative AI can be used by malicious actors is to launch data poisoning and model attacks. In the context of supply chain attacks, this could involve generating malicious content or biased recommendations, which can adversely impact supply chain decisions. CAPTCHA tools are used by websites to block bots from using their applications. These tools insist on users to complete tasks that are easy for humans, but difficult for automated systems, such as selecting objects in images or solving simple puzzles.

Advancements in Generative AI and machine learning enable bots to bypass CAPTCHA tools which can provide opportunities for gaining unauthorized access to sensitive data.[13]

Like any software, Generative AI models also can have bugs and other vulnerabilities which might cause privacy violations and wrong insights. Hence, regular security assessments of AI models must be undertaken, and appropriate security measures must be implemented to prevent any inadvertent data exposure.

Finally, new technologies raise ethical concerns regarding their deployment and usage. In the context of Generative AI, inappropriate content can be inadvertently created which might transcend ethical norms and legal boundaries. Organizations must establish guidelines for themselves as well as their supply chain partners for review of AI-generated outputs to prevent unintended consequences.

While Generative AI offers significant benefits for supply chain management, organizations must proactively address these security concerns. Robust risk assessment, mitigation strategies, strong governance, and collaboration with supply chain partners are essential for preventing supply chain attacks launched using Generative AI.

Industry 5.0 Technologies

Industry 5.0 is a transformative vision for industry that aims to create a harmonious balance between technological advancement, worker well-being, and environmental sustainability. In Industry 5.0, everything is interconnected, from smart grids to industrial factories. This vast network provides more entry points for cyber-attacks.[14] A cyber-attack on an operational environment in Industry 5.0 can bring production lines to a halt and endanger workers. From a technology advancement perspective, Industry 5.0 covers a wide spectrum of technologies that ought to work in tandem with humans across industrial systems and supply chains. These technologies and their related security concerns are detailed below:

a. Internet of Things (IoT) Devices and Robotic Automation

   IoT devices and robots are revolutionizing the way we live and work. Fascination with these technologies and their rapid adoption in the form of smart houses, smart cars drones, and automated manufacturing have often left security gaps and vulnerabilities like weak authentication, outdated firmware, and insecure communication protocols unaddressed. Data collected by IoT devices and robots could compromise user privacy if not adequately protected. Cyber-attacks on robots and drones can lead to physical harm, especially in collaborative environments where humans work alongside robots. Smart Factories rely on interconnected systems. This calls for extra security measures such as network segmentation to prevent exposing critical equipment to cyber threats.

b.   Intelligent Automation and Robotic Process Automation (RPA)

Intelligent Automation and RPA are important parts of modern supply chains to enhance supply chain agility, accuracy, and responsiveness. RPA encompasses using software robots (or "bots") to automate repetitive, rule-based tasks within business processes such as demand forecasting, order processing, supplier management, and process optimization. Hence, RPA bots interact with sensitive information such as customer data, financial records, and proprietary business information. If these bots are left unsupervised or not configured properly, they can put an organization's data at risk of being intercepted by attackers with the objective to steal, manipulate, or destroy sensitive information. Other security challenges include data leakage, fraud, logging, auditing, and access control all of which can be exploited by threat actors to disrupt supply chain operations.

c.   Drones, Unmanned Ariel Vehicles (UAVs), and other Autonomous Vehicles

Drones and UAVs depend on communication networks and software systems to operate effectively. These systems include wireless communication systems, secure transmission protocols for telemetry data (e.g., altitude, speed, battery status), and software algorithms which together control aspects like navigation, surveillance, and payload delivery. If any of these systems are compromised, it could result in unauthorized control or data leakage.

Components for drones, UAVs, and other autonomous vehicles are sourced from a supply chain that involves various manufacturers and suppliers. Securing each of these components is challenging enough. In addition, there are counterfeit components or compromised software which can introduce vulnerabilities. Security concerns include

Global Positioning System (GPS) spoofing attacks which can cause drones, UAVs, and other autonomous vehicles such as driverless cars and trucks, robo-taxis, and ships to go off course and land in unintended locations.

Companies like Aurora Innovation and their competitors are in the process of putting thousands of self-driving trucks on America's public freeways for partners like FedEx, Uber Freight, and Werner. These trucks are expected to run almost 24 × 7 hours without breaks, speeding up goods delivery, and potentially lowering costs. Among the key security concerns around autonomous vehicles related to sensor spoofing, LiDAR (Lidar sensors are a critical component in autonomous vehicles, which provides a high-resolution 3D view of their surroundings) attacks – where the sensors can be spoofed, or blinded impairing the ability to detect impacting objects, and attacks where cameras are manipulated to make wrong decisions.[15]

Threat actors can use Generative AI to manipulate navigation sensor data transmitted by ship systems. Moreover, Generative AI can also be used by them to create forged documents, such as cargo manifests, certificates of origin, or safety inspection reports.

Thus, by manipulating and tampering with sensor readings related to navigation, weather conditions, or cargo status, threat actors can deceive ship operators or automated systems to make incorrect decisions or unsafe navigation. The security of data is also at great risk as Generative AI could be used to create counterfeit digital signatures or certificates thereby compromising the authenticity of digital records, transactions, or communication.

All types of autonomous vehicles, whether on land, sea, air, or space, are assemblages of a large number of interconnected electronic components such as sensors and complex software stacks including machine learning algorithms, perception systems, and control logic sensors, applications, and communication networks. Together, these represent a large attack surface for threat actors to exploit. Ensuring the security of each component throughout the supply chain is challenging which is going to become more difficult as systems become more sophisticated and incorporate new technologies. Fixing bugs, coding errors or insecure software components, and managing over-the-air updates can provide entry points to threat actors if not securely handled. Machine learning (ML) models are also vulnerable to being manipulated by providing adversarial inputs. Protecting ML models against adversarial attacks with robust security mechanisms is crucial for safety.

d. Artificial Intelligence (AI) and Big Data Analytics

Training AI and big data analytics models requires large data sets. Preventing algorithmic biases in AI models and protecting them from adversarial attacks is critical in order to prevent manipulation or unauthorized access. Ensuring data privacy and compliance with regulations is essential.

e. Technologies Enhancing Human-Machine Interaction

Wearable devices, augmented reality (AR), and virtual reality (VR) can be vulnerable to hacking which can lead to unauthorized access, privacy breaches, and data theft. From a safety perspective AR/VR system can distract users, potentially causing accidents in industrial settings.

f. Insider Threats

Insider threats are another key area of risk. Automated supply chains which are managed and operated through human monitoring and controlling activities are at different stages and can be susceptible to insider attacks which can impact the entire production process.

The introduction of new technologies leads to the development of new standards and regulations. Compliance with these could be mandatory to gain market access. An example of this is the ISO/Society of Automotive Engineers (SAE) 21434 which is a standard that outlines cybersecurity requirements throughout the vehicle life cycle. Implementation of new standards and regulations can be challenging, but necessary to prevent a high-profile incident that can erode public trust in new technologies. Ensuring the right balance between safety measures and innovation is essential.[16]

5G Connectivity and Smart Cities

The backbone of smart cities is communication infrastructure that is driven by 5G technologies. Smart city systems are designed to collect and analyze massive volumes of data from multiple sources, including video security cameras, intelligent traffic lights, and other IoT devices, using high bandwidth, faster data transfer rates, and low latency offered by 5G technology. 5G network slicing technology can help in optimizing network performance and effective data management. Furthermore, 5G technology can enable connectivity with millions of IoT gadgets and sensors in smart cities, enabling greater coverage and real-time data processing. Hence, 5G technology is a key enabler of smart cities applications through quicker and more effective data processing while contributing to user conveniences and enhancing urban sustainability. However, 5G technologies come with their own set of vulnerabilities which also impact the operations of supply chains. The basic features of 5G which include software-defined networking, network function virtualization, mobile-access edge computing, and network slicing bring forth a new class of vulnerabilities due to their complexity and interconnectivity. In the context of supply chain operations, attack vectors such as tampering with embedded sensors and interception of real-time information in transit can be used to induce privacy, safety, and disruption risks.

6G, the next generation of mobile communication, is rapidly emerging. The timeline for its development and standardization spans from 2025 to 2029, with global release thereafter. Unlike its predecessors, 6G networks will be characterized by greater complexity, a concentration of connected devices, and heavy reliance on AI. However, this introduces new vulnerabilities, including potential attack vectors, AI-related risks, and securing extensive IoT ecosystems.[17]

Blockchain and Web3 Technology

Blockchain and Web3 technologies are already in use in select application areas and are expected to extend to a larger number of applications and industry sectors. Key characteristics of blockchain technology include decentralized, secure ledger technology, while Web3 extends this concept to create decentralized applications and ecosystems. For organizations seeking to enhance supply chain security, blockchain offers unparalleled transparency, efficiency, secure transactions and reinforces trust in supply chain processes. For example, Distributed Finance (DeFI) which leverages blockchain technology can enable counter-party risk to shift traditional credit risk to operational risk through the use of smart contracts. These programmable smart contracts automate execution and allow the creation of new financial instruments and digital assets.

While deploying blockchain technology has great potential to enhance supply chain security, it also introduces specific cybersecurity challenges. In a decentralized blockchain network, guaranteeing consistent security practices across all participants can be hard. Each participant typically is at a different level of security awareness and implementation. Having inconsistent security practices across a blockchain can weaken the overall security posture of the supply chain. Also, vulnerabilities in one participant's system can affect the entire network.

Blockchains rely on trust among participants. Here the use of self-attestation (where participants provide assurance of their own security practices) can prove to be unreliable. Any false attestation of security measures implemented could put the entire supply chain's security at risk.

Transparency which is an intrinsic feature of blockchain also exposes transaction details to all participants. Hence, sensitive information regarding pricing, contracts, intellectual property needs to be safeguarded through specific security measures. Vulnerabilities in coding flaws in smart contracts while automating processes on the blockchain can also be exploited by malicious actors to cause disruption in supply chain operations.

Another basic feature of a proof-of-work blockchain is with regard to control of the network's computing power and data integrity. Any single entity which controls more than 50% of the network's computing power can manipulate transactions. A 51% attack could alter transaction history, compromise integrity, and undermine supply chain trust.

Addressing all these risks requires a holistic approach that comprises robust security practices, standardized guidelines, and continuous monitoring. While blockchain can significantly enhance supply chain security, implementation challenges need to be overcome.

Quantum Computing

One of the most exciting and revolutionary technologies that is on the verge of making its presence felt is quantum computing (QC). While still in the laboratories, scientists and cybersecurity experts are watching its progress with bated breath. The QC sector is rapidly evolving, with new technologies, hardware, and software implementations emerging. Reports suggest that Google's quantum computer is one hundred million times faster than a personal computer.[18] This ability of quantum computers to perform complex calculations exponentially faster than classical computers opens several new vistas in areas such as materials science, pharmaceutical research, subatomic physics, logistics, and more. Quantum computing is expected to have a profound effect on AI in the coming decades as well as has applications involving cryptography, optimization, and drug discovery.

From a security standpoint, a big area of concern is that widely used present-day cryptography algorithms can be broken easily by the computing power of quantum computers. These algorithms include popular public-key cryptosystems such as Rivest-Shamir-Adleman (RSA), Elliptic Curve Cryptography (ECC) which are the foundations data of protection and secure communication are not quantum safe or quantum resistant. NIST-FIPS recommends encrypting your sensitive data with Advanced Encryption Standard (AES), a standard used by the US federal agencies to protect Secret and Top-Secret information. While AES-128 is being considered as breakable, AES-256 is still considered quantum resistant – at least until 2050.[19]

Supply chain systems are based on the continuous use of communication systems that ensure data protection. There is a real threat looming on the horizon that quantum computers can disrupt supply chains and impact materials, components, sub-assemblies, or QC-related goods and services. Unauthorized quantum-powered access to key raw materials information and manufacturing/assembly equipment can be a significant concern. Establishing a stable supply chain that can meet the new threats emerging from quantum computing requires specific assessment of risk scenarios by organizations that are based on a post-quantum computing era. Organizations need to implement strong encryption, access controls, and data privacy measures that are quantum resistant.

The Impact of New Regulations, Standards, and Frameworks

Managing supply chain cyber risks is indeed a complex endeavor, and the introduction of new technologies can exacerbate the challenge by introducing additional vulnerabilities. This emphasizes the fact that organizations must be proactive in safeguarding their supply chains against cyber threats. Important sources of guidance on managing supply chain risks are available from the National Institute of Standards and Technology (NIST), which has recently updated its foundational Cybersecurity Supply Chain Risk Management (C-SCRM) guidance.[20] This guidance contains key practices for identifying, assessing, and responding to cybersecurity risks throughout the supply chain.[21] It highlights the need to move focus from just the finished product to its components and on tasks and activities in their journey to the destination. The updated publication, titled "Cybersecurity Supply Chain Risk Management Practices for Systems and Organizations," was prepared in response to the White House Executive Order 14028, which aims to enhance the security of the software supply chain.

Likewise, the adoption of new FAR Rules on Cybersecurity and Supply Chains which contain new security-related requirements for federal contractors such as protection of controlled unclassified information, reporting of threats and incidents to government, prohibition of certain types of information and communication technology purchases as well as continuous monitoring requirements for cloud services is a useful way of building robust supply chain security.

The Department of Homeland Security (DHS) has also proposed regulations to improve supply chain resilience and cybersecurity. These regulations encompass various cybersecurity measures, including account security, device security, network segmentation, data security, training, incident response planning, and drills and exercises.

It is true that by implementing these practices or drawing from them, organizations can enhance their capability to manage cybersecurity risks within and across their supply chains. However, complying with new standards and regulations can be challenging for organizations due to the following reasons:

1. In a constantly evolving technology landscape, regulations also continually evolve to address changing threats and privacy concerns. Keeping up with these changes, evaluating their implications requires constant attention on the status and changes in standards and regulations.

2. Organizations need to identify all applicable laws and regulations that affect their business. There are a range of local, federal, state, and industry regulations that demand compliance. When an organization's operations are spread across multiple jurisdictions, involve industry-specific requirements relating to their supply chain, the task becomes more complex.

3. Small businesses often lack in-house compliance expertise. With limited resources at their disposal, it is difficult for them to understand and implement controls and procedures to comply with laws and regulations in time. Non-compliance could lead to financial penalties and reputational damage.

Just like the supply chain cyber threat environment is continuously changing, the regulatory and standards environment is also dynamic. Organizations must navigate this complex landscape which could extend beyond their boundaries to their supply chain partners, allocate resources, and stay informed to avoid penalties and maintain trust of all stakeholders.

Developing and Adopting an Approach to Safeguard Supply Chains against Cyber Risks

In supply chain cyber risk management, organizations often do not know where to start. Effective supply chain cyber risk management involves several key practices. Here are ten essential tenets that can help in developing an approach and strategy for effectively managing supply chain cyber risks:

1. Integrate C-SCRM practices into all aspects of your organization including procurement, vendor management, and operational processes.
2. Build a supply chain cyber risk management framework. Develop a structured program specifically focused on managing cyber risks within your supply chain including clear definition of roles, responsibilities, and processes.
3. Identify critical components and suppliers in your supply chain. Prioritize risk assessments and mitigation efforts for these key partners.
4. Develop a comprehensive understanding of your supply chain, including dependencies, interconnections, and potential vulnerabilities.
5. Ensure continuous visibility into the supply chain. Visibility is critical for tracking components, suppliers, and processes.
6. Implement threat management by identifying, assessing, and mitigating risks posed by potential threats to your supply chain. Conduct regular risk assessments to understand vulnerabilities. Implement security controls to prevent and detect threats. Put in place incident response plans to address threats promptly.

7. Engage suppliers in cybersecurity training, resilience planning, addressing vulnerabilities to enhance overall supply chain security.
8. Ensure that critical suppliers are in sync with organization's cyber risk management strategy and efforts on an ongoing basis.
9. Assess supplier security practices throughout the supplier relationship period and monitor their adherence to security requirements.
10. Follow and comply with standards and regulations for supply chain security. Regularly review and update compliance policies, monitor changes in regulations, and adjust practices accordingly.

Supply chain cyber risk management is an ongoing effort that requires collaboration, adaptability, and a comprehensive approach. Setting up a robust governance mechanism to periodically review supply chain cyber risks, implementing required controls, and mitigating actions is key to improve resilience and ability of the supply chain in responding to threats. The effectiveness of such a governance mechanism can only be ensured by involving supply chain participants and maintaining close collaboration on an ongoing basis.

Notes

1   Statista. (2024, March 26). U.S. number of supply chain attacks 2017–2023. https://www.statista.com/statistics/1367189/us-annual-number-of-supply-chain-attacks/.
2   Us, J. K. W. (2024, March 7). Data breaches increased in 2023 and with them, internet security concerns. *The Week.* https://theweek.com/tech/data-breaches-increase-2023-internet-security-concerns.
3   Freeze, D. (2023, October 3). Software supply chain attacks to cost the world $60 billion by 2025. *Cybercrime Magazine.* https://cybersecurityventures.com/software-supply-chain-attacks-to-cost-the-world-60-billion-by-2025/.
4   Welburn, J. (2021, June 22). Supply chains have a cyber problem. RAND. https://www.rand.org/pubs/commentary/2021/06/supply-chains-have-a-cyber-problem.html.
5   The MOVEit breach impact and fallout: How can you respond? (2023, July 19). Security Intelligence. https://securityintelligence.com/news/the-moveit-breach-impact-and-fallout-how-can-you-respond/.
6   PaperCut security post-incident report from April 2023. (n.d.). *PaperCut.* https://www.papercut.com/blog/news/security-post-incident-report-april-2023/.
7   Kapko, M. (2024, March 26). Phishing remains top route to initial access. *Cybersecurity Dive.* https://www.cybersecuritydive.com/news/phishing-initial-access-cyber-attack/711371/.
8   Statista. (2024, March 26). U.S. number of supply chain attacks 2017–2023. https://www.statista.com/statistics/1367189/us-annual-number-of-supply-chain-attacks/.

9   Aguilera, A. (2024, May 26). AI vs generative AI: What's the difference? *MyCase*. https://www.mycase.com/blog/ai/ai-vs-Generative-ai/.
10   Kelley, D., & Kelley, D. (2023, July 13). WormGPT – The generative AI tool cyber-criminals are using to launch BEC attacks|SlashNext. SlashNext|Complete generative AI security for email, mobile, and browser. https://slashnext.com/blog/wormgpt-the-Generative-ai-tool-cybercriminals-are-using-to-launch-business-email-compromise-attacks/.
11   Sjouwerman, S. (2024, February 20). Deepfake phishing: the dangerous new face of cybercrime. *Forbes*. https://www.forbes.com/sites/forbestechcouncil/2024/01/23/deepfake-phishing-the-dangerous-new-face-of-cybercrime/?sh=20017a3f4aed.
12   Kumar, V., & Bfsi, E. (2024, April 17). How deepfake videos can pose financial risk? Experts suggest safety tips. ETBFSI.com. https://bfsi.economictimes.indiatimes.com/news/financial-services/how-deepfake-videos-can-pose-financial-risk-experts-suggest-safety-tips/109354640.
13   What cybersecurity threats does Generative AI expose us to? (2023, July 31). World Economic Forum. https://www.weforum.org/agenda/2023/06/what-cybersecurity-threats-are-posed-by-Generative-ai/.
14   Cybersecurity and the 5th Industrial Revolution: Why you shouldn't ignore it! (n.d.). https://www.marketsandmarkets.com/blog/ICT/Cybersecurity-and-the-5th-Industrial-Revolution-Why-you-shouldnt-ignore-it.
15   R Street Institute. (2024, April 28). Addressing new challenges in automotive cyber-security. R Street Institute. https://www.rstreet.org/research/addressing-new-challenges-in-automotive-cybersecurity/.
16   Krisher, T. (2024, April 29). The future is near for self-driving trucks on US roads. *AP News*. https://apnews.com/article/trucks-selfdriving-highways-automation-driver-083409631158f54d806d75309c4764e2.
17   Remmert, H. (n.d.). When is 6G coming, and what does it mean for 5G and 4G LTE? Digi. https://www.digi.com/blog/post/when-is-6g-coming-what-does-it-mean-for-5g-4g.
18   Reynolds, E. (2015, December 9). Google's quantum computer works, it says. WIRED. https://www.wired.com/story/google-quantum-computing-d-wave/.
19   McNeely, D. (2024, February 13). Transitioning to Quantum-Safe encryption. Delinea. https://delinea.com/blog/quantum-safe-encryption.
20   Boyens, J., Smith, A., Bartol, N., Winkler, K., Holbrook, A., & Fallon, M. (2022). Cybersecurity Supply chain risk management practices for systems and organizations. In NIST Special Publication. U.S. Department of Commerce. https://nvlpubs.nist.gov/nistpubs/SpecialPublications/NIST.SP.800-161r1.pdf.
21   New EO Guidance for Cybersecurity Supply Chain Risk Management (2022, May 6). NIST. https://www.nist.gov/news-events/news/2022/05/new-eo-guidance-cybersecurity-supply-chain-risk-management.

APPENDIX

THIRD-PARTY RELATIONSHIPS: INTERAGENCY GUIDANCE ON RISK MANAGEMENT

Introduction: 2023 Interagency Guidance on Third-Party Relationships

Risk Management was issued on June 6, 2023 by the Office of the Comptroller of the Currency (OCC), the Federal Reserve, and the Federal Deposit Insurance Corporation.[1] The guidance applies to all banks with third-party relationships, including Community Banks and supersedes previous OCC bulletins.

Scope of Business Arrangements

Previously, there was some ambiguity if scope of third-party management programs should be limited to only contractual vendor relationships. The new guidance clarifies that all business arrangements are potentially in scope of oversight and may include customers or arrangements without direct contractual obligations.[2]

This guidance addresses any business arrangement between a banking organization and another entity, by contract or otherwise. A third-party relationship may exist despite a lack of a contract or remuneration. Third-party relationships can include, but are not limited to, outsourced services, use of independent consultants, referral arrangements, merchant payment processing services, services provided by affiliates and subsidiaries, and joint ventures.[2]

Implications of this clarification may significantly increase scope of third-party risk perimeter that needs to be monitored by banks.

Considerations for Managing Foreign Third Parties

The agencies have included a footnote to address questions surrounding the term "foreign-based third party" and included considerations for foreign-based third parties within relevant sections of the risk management life cycle.

In contracts with foreign-based third parties, it is important to consider choice-of-law and jurisdictional provisions that provide dispute adjudication under the laws of a single jurisdiction, whether in the United States or elsewhere. When engaging with foreign-based third parties or where contracts include a choice-of-law provision that includes a jurisdiction other than the United States, it is important to understand that such contracts and covenants may be subject to the interpretation of foreign courts relying on laws in those jurisdictions. It may be warranted to seek legal advice on the enforceability of the proposed contract with a foreign-based third party and other legal ramifications, including privacy laws and cross-border flow of information.[2]

It provides an important intersection of how management of third parties intersects with data privacy and cross-border programs.

Clarification for Managing "FinTechs" and Other Types of Vendors

The guidance specifically calls out that management of FinTechs or affiliates should not follow alternative approaches or assume lower levels of risk.

It is important for a banking organization to understand how the arrangement with a third party, including a FinTech company, is structured so that the banking organization may assess the types and levels of risks posed and determine how to manage those third-party relationships accordingly.[2]

Agencies added specific considerations to highlight unique risks with these types of third parties.

Clarification on Usage of Industry Vendor Risk Assessment Utilities

Agencies clarified usage of assessment industry utilities and/or collaborative efforts we covered in a previous chapter.

With respect to commenters focused on steps to limit the burdens of due diligence, including collaboration with other banking organizations, and engaging with third parties that specialize in conducting due diligence, the agencies note that such collaborative efforts could be beneficial and reduce burden, especially for community banking organizations and have made certain clarifying revisions to the guidance in that regard. However, use of any collaborative efforts does not abrogate the responsibility of banking organizations to manage third-party relationships in a safe and sound manner and consistent with applicable laws and regulations (including antitrust laws). It is important for the banking organization to evaluate the conclusions from such collaborative efforts.[2]

This guidance further confirmed that using a risk assessment utility is actually a business arrangement that needs to go through its own vendor due diligence cycle.

Clarification on Subcontracts Definitions and Oversight

Agencies provided important clarifications on usage of subcontractors and the need to assess whether additional risk is presented by the geographic location of a subcontractor or dependency on a single provider for multiple activities. That requires more sophistication for measuring concentration risk across the entire third- and fourth-party portfolio.

Clarification of Management vs Board Responsibilities

The agencies have made changes to clarify and distinguish the board's responsibilities from management's responsibilities and to avoid the appearance of a prescriptive approach to the board's role in the risk management life cycle, while still emphasizing that the board has ultimate oversight responsibility to ensure that the banking organization operates in a safe and sound manner and in compliance with applicable laws and regulations.[2]

In practical terms, that aligns with an overall model for three Lines of Defense, ensuring that the board provides appropriate oversight and challenge.

Emphasis on Skills Requirement

Given the diverse nature of third-party relationships, ensuring appropriate skills from both the banks and third parties is a critical success factor. Agencies highlighted that importance as part of this guidance.

Banks: It is important to involve staff with the requisite knowledge and skills in each stage of the risk management life cycle. A banking organization may involve experts across disciplines, such as compliance, risk, or technology, as well as legal counsel and may engage external support when helpful to supplement the qualifications and technical expertise of in-house staff.[2]

Thirty Parties: An evaluation of a third party's: (1) depth of resources (including staffing); (2) previous experience in performing the activity; and (3) history of addressing customer complaints or litigation and subsequent outcomes helps to inform a banking organization's assessment of the third party's ability to perform the activity effectively.[2]

Management of Information Systems

Agencies highlighted the importance of understanding a third party's control environment when technology is involved as part of a service. That technology can be used either directly or indirectly in service fulfillment.

When technology is a major component of the third-party relationship, an effective practice is to review both the banking organization's and the third party's information systems to identify gaps in service-level expectations, business process and management, and interoperability issues. It is also important to review the third party's processes for maintaining timely and accurate inventories of its technology and its contractor(s). A banking organization also benefits from understanding the third party's measures for assessing the performance of its information systems.[2]

Operational Resilience

There is an important overlap of third-party risk with operational resilience and the agency integrated operational resilience considerations throughout their guidance.

Some considerations related to operational resilience include (1) dependency on a single provider for multiple activities and (2) interoperability or potential end-of-life issues with the software programming language, computer platform, or data storage technologies used by the third party.[2]

To help ensure maintenance of operations, contracts often require the third party to provide the banking organization with operating procedures to be carried out in the event business continuity plans are implemented, including specific recovery time and recovery point objectives. Contracts may also stipulate whether and how often the banking organization and the third party will jointly test business continuity plans. Another consideration is whether the contract provides for the transfer of the banking organization's accounts, data, or activities to another third party without penalty in the event of the third party's bankruptcy, business failure, or business interruption.[2]

Contract Negotiations Expectations

Agencies added a detailed section on contract negotiations expectations. This section aligns with Chapter 15 where we outline the top 10 contract considerations.

Specifically, agencies call out a need for the right to audit, remediation requirements, monitoring laws and regulations, cost clarifications, and ensuring that contracts do not include incentives that promote inappropriate risk-taking.

Notes

1   "OCC Bulletin 2023-17 Third-Party Relationships: Interagency Guidance on Risk Management", OCC, June 6, 2023, https://www2.occ.gov/news-issuances/bulletins/2023/bulletin-2023-17.html.
2   "Interagency Guidance on Third-Party Relationships: Risk Management", Federal Register National Archives, June 6, 2023, https://www.federalregister.gov/documents/2023/06/09/2023-12340/interagency-guidance-on-third-party-relationships-risk-management.

INDEX

Note: **Bold** page numbers refer to tables and *italic* page numbers refer to figures.

For Product Safety Concerns and Information please contact our EU
representative GPSR@taylorandfrancis.com
Taylor & Francis Verlag GmbH, Kaufingerstraße 24, 80331 München, Germany